Combating Crime in the Digital Age: a Critical Review of EU Information Systems in the Area of Freedom, Security and Justice in the Post-Interoperability Era

Transnational Crime

Volumes published in this Brill Research Perspective are listed at *brill.com/rptc*

Combating Crime in the Digital Age: a Critical Review of EU Information Systems in the Area of Freedom, Security and Justice in the Post-Interoperability Era

Challenges for Criminal Law and Personal Data Protection

By

Athina Giannakoula
Dafni Lima
Maria Kaiafa-Gbandi

BRILL

LEIDEN | BOSTON

Originally published as Volume 2(4) in *Transnational Crime*, DOI:10.1163/24680931-12340010.

Library of Congress Control Number: 2020932442

Typeface for the Latin, Greek, and Cyrillic scripts: "Brill". See and download: brill.com/brill-typeface.

ISBN 978-90-04-42522-4 (paperback)
ISBN 978-90-04-42523-1 (e-book)

This book is printed on acid-free paper and produced in a sustainable manner.

Contents

Combating Crime in the Digital Age: a Critical Review of EU Information Systems in the Area of Freedom, Security and Justice in the Post-Interoperability Era

Challenges for Criminal Law and Personal Data Protection

Athina Giannakoula
Aristotle University of Thessaloniki
athgiann@law.auth.gr

Dafni Lima
Aristotle University of Thessaloniki
dafni.lima@cantab.net

Maria Kaiafa-Gbandi
Aristotle University of Thessaloniki
kaiafagb@law.auth.gr

Abstract

This article provides a systematic and critical account of EU information systems in the area of freedom, security and justice, with the aim of establishing the contemporary links between information sharing and criminal law in the EU and of evaluating its impact on individuals. To this end, Part 1 offers a systemisation and critical assessment of the essential elements of the pertinent systems (ECRIS, ECRIS-TCN, Prüm, PNR, Europol, SIS, Eurodac, VIS, EES, ETIAS) and of the new interoperability regime under Regulation (EU) 2019/818, from the perspective of their objective to prevent and combat serious crime and to ensure a high level of security in the EU. In Part 2 the article explores personal data protection law, police law and criminal procedure law, in order to propose safeguards and limitations for effectively regulating this rapidly evolving framework and addressing the growing challenges for fundamental legal principles and individual rights. In this respect, the authors put forward concrete views and ideas, on the basis of their central suggestion that the issue discussed falls within the context of an emerging *precognitive* paradigm of criminal law.

 | DOI:10.1163/9789004425231_002

Keywords

European criminal law – principle of proportionality – presumption of innocence – EU information systems – personal data – Interoperability Regulation (EU) 2019/818 – area of freedom, security and justice

Introduction*

In recent years, gathering and exchanging personal data has evolved into an integral part of the effort of the EU to ensure a high level of *security* for its citizens.[1] As terrorism and organised crime, the two types of criminal activity that are of great gravity and central significance to EU law in the area of freedom, security and justice, are constantly *transforming*—mainly *by taking advantage of new technologies* and becoming more complex in some cases, or by losing some of their sophistication and traditional identifying characteristics

* The research 'Combating crime in the digital age: new technologies in the service of security and challenges for personal data protection—a systematic and critical review of the EU and Greek legislation' (MIS 5005203) is implemented through the Operational Program 'Human Resources Development, Education and Lifelong Learning' 2014–2020 and is co-financed by the European Union (European Social Fund) and Greek national funds. This article was written in 2019 by Athina Giannakoula, Postdoctoral Researcher at the Aristotle University and Lecturer at the National School for Judges of Greece, and Dafni Lima, PhD Candidate and Scholar of the Academy of Athens and of the Fulbright Foundation, under the advisory supervision and guidance of Maria Kaiafa-Gbandi, Professor of Criminal Law at the Aristotle University of Thessaloniki, and was published in 2020.

1 See Commission, 'The European Agenda on Security' (Communication) COM (2015) 185, 5ff; Commission, 'Stronger and Smarter Information Systems for Borders and Security' (Communication) COM (2016) 205. Also Deirdre Curtin 'Security of the Interstice and Interoperable Data Sharing: A First Cut' in Sergio Carrera and Valsamis Mitsilegas (eds), *Constitutionalising the Security Union* (CEPS 2017) (*Constitutionalising*) 65. For more on EU criminal law and policy, see inter alia Anne Weyembergh, 'History of the Cooperation' in Roberto E. Kostoris (ed), *Handbook on European criminal procedure* (Springer 2018) (*Handbook criminal procedure*) 174–196; Roberto E. Kostoris, 'European Law and Criminal Justice' in *Handbook criminal procedure* 4ff; Helmut Satzger, *International and European Criminal Law* (2nd edn, Beck 2018) 45ff; André Klip, *European Criminal Law* (Intersentia 2016); Petter Asp, *The Procedural Criminal Law Cooperation of the EU* (Stockholm University 2016) 39ff; Bernd Hecker, *Europäisches Strafrecht* (Springer 2015); Maria Kaiafa-Gbandi and Theodoros Papakyriakou, *Elements of EU Criminal Law* [in Greek] (2nd edn, Sakkoulas 2019); Athina Giannakoula, *Crime and Sanctions in the European Union* [in Greek] (Nomiki Bibliothiki 2015) 3ff; Henri Labayale, 'The institutional framework' in Valsamis Mitsilegas, Maria Bergström and Theodore Konstadinides (eds), *Research Handbook on EU Criminal Law* (Elgar 2016) (*Research Handbook*) 29–48; Rosaria Sicurella 'EU competence in criminal matters' in *Research Handbook* 49–77.

in others—,[2] combating serious crime is a growing challenge in the EU. In view of the above and of the apparent necessity for law enforcement authorities to employ technology themselves, it is no surprise that, at a time where massive amounts of data can be easily collected and stored, *information* is perceived as an invaluable tool for *detecting* and even *preventing* crime. To this end, the EU has developed a series of legal instruments and processes that regulate the collecting, processing and sharing of personal data, including several information systems.[3]

At an institutional level, in April 2015, the European Agenda on Security[4] was issued reinforcing the objectives set out in the previous EU Internal Security Strategy (2010–2014)[5] and paving the way for the renewed Internal Security Strategy (2015–2020).[6] Both the European Agenda on Security and

2 For example, online criminality in the form of organised crime, fraud and even terrorism rises worldwide, thus becoming difficult to detect and combat; at the same time, criminal organisations lose their traditional structures and function within frameworks that are much more difficult to dismantle, while terrorist attacks are spreading through the choice of less symbolic (and thus easier to reach) targets and the use of simple objects as weapons. See indicatively the Europol Reports 'Internet Organised Crime Threat Assessment 2018' <www.europol.europa.eu/internet-organised-crime-threat-assessment-2018>, 'Terrorism Situation and Trend Report 2019 (TE-SAT)' <www.europol.europa.eu/activities-services/main-reports/terrorism-situation-and-trend-report-2019-te-sat>, 'The threat from terrorism in the EU became more complex in 2018' <www.europol.europa.eu/newsroom/news/threat-terrorism-in-eu-became-more-complex-in-2018> and 'Europol Review 2016–2017' <www.europol.europa.eu/activities-services/main-reports/europol-review-2016–2017> all accessed 1 February 2020.

3 Jörg Eisele 'Datenverkehr und Datenschutz im Rahmen der polizeilichen und justiziellen Zusammenarbeit' in Max-Planck-Institut für ausländisches und internationales Strafrecht and others (eds), *Europäisches Strafrecht* (Nomos Verlag 2014) 877–900; Ángeles Gutiérrez Zarza, *Exchange of Information and Data Protection in Cross-border Criminal Proceedings in Europe* (Springer 2015) 117–140; Despoina Anagnostopoulou (ed), *Developments and challenges of the EU area of freedom, security and justice: proceedings of the International Conference in the memory of Dimitrios Evrigenis* (University of Macedonia Press 2015) ch 1–3; Valsamis Mitsilegas, 'The Security Union as a Paradigm of Preventive Justice: Challenges for Citizenship, Fundamental Rights and the Rule of Law' in *Constitutionalising* 7ff; Virginia Tzortzi, *Personal Data Protection in the Area of Freedom, Security and Justice* [in Greek] (Nomiki Bibliothiki 2018) 96ff; Maria Kaiafa-Gbandi, 'Information Exchange for the Purpose of Crime Control: the EU Paradigm for Controlling Terrorism—Challenges of an "Open" System for Collecting and Exchanging Personal Data' [2019] European Criminal Law Review (EuCLR) 141.

4 COM (2015) 185. Also, Athina Giannakoula, 'The European Agenda on Security—A Comment' [2016] EuCLR 99.

5 Commission, 'The EU Internal Security Strategy in Action: Five steps towards a more secure Europe' (Communication) COM (2010) 673.

6 See Council, 'Draft Council Conclusions on the Renewed European Union Internal Security Strategy 2015–2020', 9798/15.

the subsequent Progress Reports 'towards an effective and genuine Security Union'[7] have highlighted the use and exchange of personal data in the context of preventing and combating crime. Better information exchange constitutes the first pillar of EU action in the Agenda,[8] which defines terrorism, serious and organised cross-border crime, and cybercrime as the three priorities for EU security.[9] Recently, the EU's efforts in the area have culminated in introducing *interoperability*[10] across selected information systems, which will result in considerable changes both in how the data can be accessed and in the relevant powers of law enforcement authorities.

In view of the above, the present contribution examines *the EU information systems related to* ***security*** as a constituent element of the area of freedom, security and justice and as an EU objective under EU primary law. In accordance with this criterion, it concerns the information systems which, on the one hand, *are based on provisions of Chapters 4 and 5 of Title V of the Third Part of the Treaty on the Functioning of the EU* (TFEU) and, on the other hand, were included *either in the European Agenda on Security of 2015 or in the Commission's legislative proposal on interoperability*,[11] i.e. in documents of central importance for the establishment and the evolution of personal data collection, processing and sharing within the area of freedom, security and justice. Hence, the study deals with legislative acts which fall under a *common* institutional framework (= the one consisting of judicial cooperation in criminal matters and of police cooperation) and is particularly *topical*, given that it follows relevant contemporary developments.

More specifically, the study examines:[12]

---

7 The reports are available at https://ec.europa.eu/home-affairs/what-we-do/policies/european-agenda-security/legislative-documents_en.

8 COM (2015) 185, 5.

9 COM (2015) 185, 12ff.

10 Regulation (EU) 2019/818 of 20 May 2019 on establishing a framework for interoperability between EU information systems in the field of police and judicial cooperation, asylum and migration and amending Regulations (EU) 2018/1726, (EU) 2018/1862 and (EU) 2019/816 [2019] OJ L135/85 (Interoperability Regulation).

11 See the original Commission, 'Proposal for a Regulation on establishing a framework for interoperability between EU information systems for police and judicial cooperation, asylum and migration' COM (2017) 794 (Interoperability Proposal).

12 The legislative framework presented is updated till 7 February 2020. The EU primary law provisions serving as legal bases for each legal act are cited in square brackets.

- the European Criminal Records Information System (ECRIS),[13]
- the ECRIS for Third Country Nationals (ECRIS-TCN),[14]
- the Prüm framework,[15]
- the Passenger Name Records (PNR) framework,[16]
- the Europol system,[17]
- the Schengen Information System (SIS),[18]
- the European Dactyloscopy (Eurodac) system,[19]

---

13 Framework Decision 2008/675/JHA of 24 July 2008 on taking account of convictions in the Member States of the EU in the course of new criminal proceedings [2008] OJ L 220/32 [arts 31, 34(2)(b) ex TEU]; Framework Decision 2009/315/JHA of 26 February 2009 on the organisation and content of the exchange of information extracted from the criminal record between Member States [2009] OJ L 93/23 (*ECRIS FD*) [arts 31, 34(2)(b) ex TEU]; Council Decision 2009/316/JHA of 6 April 2009 on the establishment of the European Criminal Records Information System (ECRIS) in application of Article 11 of Framework Decision 2009/315/JHA [2009] OJ L 93/33 [arts 31, 34(2)(c) ex TEU]; Directive (EU) 2019/884 of 17 April 2019 amending Framework Decision 2009/315/JHA and replacing Council Decision 2009/316/JHA [2019] OJ L 151/143 (*ECRIS Directive*) [art 82(1)(d) TFEU].

14 Regulation (EU) 2019/816 of 17 April 2019 establishing a centralised system for the identification of Member States holding conviction information on third-country nationals and stateless persons (ECRIS-TCN) to supplement the ECRIS and amending Regulation (EU) 2018/1726 [2019] OJ L 135/1 (ECRIS-TCN Regulation) [art 82(1)(d) TFEU].

15 Council Decision 2008/615/JHA of 23 June 2008 on the stepping up of cross-border cooperation, particularly in combating terrorism and cross-border crime [2008] OJ L 210/1 (*Prüm Decision*) [arts 30(1)(a),(b), 31(1)(a), 32, 34(2)(c) ex TEU].

16 Directive (EU) 2016/681 of 27 April 2016 on the use of passenger name record (PNR) data for the prevention, detection, investigation and prosecution of terrorist offences and serious crime [2016] OJ L 119/132 (*PNR Directive*) [art 82(1)(d), 87(2)(a) TFEU].

17 Regulation (EU) 2016/794 of 11 May 2016 on the European Union Agency for Law Enforcement Cooperation (Europol) [2016] OJ L 135/53 (*Europol Regulation*) [art 88 TFEU].

18 Council Decision 2007/533/JHA of 12 June 2007 on the establishment, operation and use of the second generation Schengen Information System (SIS II) [2007] OJ L 205/63 (SIS II Decision) [arts 30(1)(a),(b), 31(1)(a),(b), 34(2)(c) ex TEU]; Regulation (EU) 2018/1862 of 28 November 2018 on the establishment, operation and use of the Schengen Information System (SIS) in the field of police cooperation and judicial cooperation in criminal matters, amending and repealing Council Decision 2007/533/JHA, and repealing Regulation (EC) No 1986/2006 and Commission Decision 2010/261/EU [2018] OJ L 312/56 (*SIS Regulation*) [arts 82(1), 85(1), 87(2)(a), 88(2)(a) TFEU].

19 Regulation (EU) No 603/2013 of 26 June 2013 on the establishment of 'Eurodac' for the comparison of fingerprints for the effective application of Regulation (EU) No 604/2013 and on requests for the comparison with Eurodac data by Member States' law enforcement authorities and Europol for law enforcement purposes, and amending Regulation (EU) No 1077/2011 [2013] OJ L 180/1 (*Eurodac Regulation*) [arts 78(2)(e), 87(2)(a), 88(2)(a) TFEU]; Regulation (EU) 2018/1726 of 14 November 2018 on the European Union Agency for the Operational Management of Large-Scale IT Systems in the Area of Freedom, Security and Justice (eu-LISA), and amending Regulation (EC) No 1987/2006 and Council

- the Visa Information System (VIS),[20]
- the Entry/Exit System (EES),[21] and
- the European Travel Information and Authorisation System (ETIAS).[22]

On the contrary, also in accordance with the abovementioned criteria, this study does not deal with data collecting or sharing performed by *non-EU* organisations (e.g. Interpol). Moreover, it does not cover any EU data collecting or sharing procedures which are *exclusively linked to specific activities and criminal offences* (e.g. drug trafficking,[23] using the financial system for money laundering,[24]

Decision 2007/533/JHA and repealing Regulation (EU) No 1077/2011 [2018] OJ L 295/99 [arts 74, 77(2)(a),(b), 78(2)(e), 79(2)(c), 82(1)(d), 85(1), 87(2)(a) 88(2) TFEU]; Commission, 'Proposal for a Regulation on the establishment of "Eurodac" for the comparison of fingerprints for the effective application of [Regulation (EU) No 604/2013], for identifying an illegally staying third-country national or stateless person and on requests for the comparison with Eurodac data by Member States' law enforcement authorities and Europol for law enforcement purposes' COM (2016) 272 [arts 78(2)(e), 79(2)(c), 87(2)(a), 88(2)(a) TFEU].

20 Council Decision 2008/633/JHA of 23 June 2008 concerning access for consultation of the Visa Information System (VIS) by designated authorities of Member States and by Europol for the purposes of the prevention, detection and investigation of terrorist offences and of other serious criminal offences [2008] OJ L 218/129 (*VIS Decision*) [arts 30(1)(b), 31(1)(a),(b), 34(2)(c) ex TEU]; Commission, 'Proposal for a Regulation amending Regulation (EC) No 767/2008, Regulation (EC) No 810/2009, Regulation (EU) 2017/2226, Regulation (EU) 2016/399, Regulation XX/2018 [Interoperability Regulation], and Decision 2004/512/EC and repealing Council Decision 2008/633/JHA' COM (2018) 302 [Arts 16(2), 77(2)(a),(b),(d),(e), 78(2)(d),(e),(g), 79(2)(c),(d), 87(2)(a), 88(2)(a) TFEU].

21 Regulation (EU) 2017/2226 of 30 November 2017 establishing an Entry/Exit System (EES) to register entry and exit data and refusal of entry data of third-country nationals crossing the external borders of the Member States and determining the conditions for access to the EES for law enforcement purposes, and amending the Convention implementing the Schengen Agreement and Regulations (EC) No 767/2008 and (EU) No 1077/2011 [2017] OJ L 327/20 (*EES Regulation*) [arts 77(2)(b),(c), 87(2)(a) TFEU].

22 Regulation (EU) 2018/1240 of 12 September 2018 establishing a European Travel Information and Authorisation System (ETIAS) and amending Regulations (EU) No 1077/2011, (EU) No 515/2014, (EU) 2016/399, (EU) 2016/1624 and (EU) 2017/2226 [2018] OJ L 236/1 (*ETIAS Regulation*) [arts 77(2)(b),(d), 87(2)(a) TFEU].

23 See Regulation (EC) No 1920/2006 of 12 December 2006 on the European Monitoring Centre for Drugs and Drug Addiction [2006] OJ L 376/1 [art 152 Treaty establishing the European Community (TEC)].

24 See Directive (EU) 2015/849 of 20 May 2015 on the prevention of the use of the financial system for the purposes of money laundering or terrorist financing, amending Regulation (EU) No 648/2012 and repealing Directive 2005/60/EC and Directive 2006/70/EC [2015] OJ L 141/73 [art 114 TFEU].

regulating customs and agricultural matters[25]), because these are founded on legal bases falling outside the scope of the area of freedom, security and justice, and each one of them has a distinct structure, depending on the needs deriving from the criminal offence or activity it relates to.[26]

Part 1. Systematic Approach on the Information Systems Employed for the Purpose of Preventing and Combating Serious Crime within the Area of Freedom, Security and Justice

Against this background, to understand the features and the function of the systems examined, and to pinpoint the most significant issues to analyse and critically assess in Part 2, the following sections present and comment on: the fundamental elements of each system (1), a systematic selection of certain elements which are essential from a criminal law perspective (2), the estimated effect of the interoperability of the systems (3) and the key traits of the Greek rules implementing the respective EU legislative acts as an example of national legislation (4).

25 See Council Regulation (EC) No 515/97 on mutual assistance between the administrative authorities of the Member States and cooperation between the latter and the Commission to ensure the correct application of the law on customs and agricultural matters [1997] OJ L 82/1 [arts 43 and 235 TEC] concerning the functioning of the Customs Information System.

26 For example, the information collected by the European Monitoring Centre for Drugs and Drug Addiction pursues quite different objectives, as it aims to provide Member States with 'actual, objective, reliable and comparable information at European level concerning drugs and drug addiction and their consequences'; it includes 'data resulting from research, communicated by Member States and data emanating from Community, non-governmental national sources and competent international organisations', it refers to treatment, infectious diseases, social concerns, statistics of drug use, best practices in the Member States, emerging trends in poly-drug use etc., and (among other functions) it is to be used to facilitate 'exchanges of information between decision-makers, researchers, specialists and those involved in drugs-related issues in governmental and non-governmental organisations' [see arts 1(2) and 2(2) of Regulation (EC) No 1920/2006 and the Statistical Bulletin 2019 <www.emcdda.europa.eu/data/stats2019_en> accessed 1 February 2020]. On the other hand, but also structured in a unique manner, the data collection and sharing that aims to *prevent* the use of the EU's financial system for the purposes of money laundering and terrorist financing is conducted based on an set of elaborate obligations on numerous natural and legal persons to provide information, which thus dictate the content (or at least part of it) of daily activities (eg bank transactions and various other business or financial procedures, consulting with lawyers) and the internal operation of corporations.

1 *The Systems Falling under the Scope of the Research Project: a Concise Overview of Their Scope and Objective*

This section presents the most significant of the constituent elements of the systems included in the study. More specifically, it provides similar information for each system, so as to achieve a concise overview of their function as a whole, but also to enable a comparative approach on the EU's data collecting and sharing mechanisms. To this extent, it mainly refers to certain fundamental categories of elements, such as the principal objective of each system, its structure, the persons affected and the personal data collected. Given the criminal law perspective of this study, the systems are primarily classified in view of their central or decentralised structure (as the former are more intrusive than the latter) and their degree of connection to criminal law. The following overview also takes into account the different context within which each system operates, pointing out which systems are established under judicial cooperation in criminal matters or police cooperation, and which systems mainly focus on border controls.

1.1 Decentralised Systems

The decentralised systems examined in this paper share a common feature, as they are all intrinsically connected to criminal law. The *Prüm Framework*[27] is arguably the one connected more strongly with criminal law both in terms of data collected and of its objectives, as it focuses on data collected in the context of criminal proceedings and regulates information exchange for the purposes of combating terrorism and cross-border crime or safeguarding public order and security during broadly defined 'major events'.[28] It was established within judicial cooperation for EU Member States, connecting national databases. Even though it is technically a decentralised system, Prüm is arguably the most intrusive one, as it gives the user direct access to all national Prüm databases across Member States. *ECRIS* was also formed in the context of judicial cooperation[29] as a decentralised system aiming to

27 In 2005, the Prüm Convention was adopted, aiming at enhancing cross-border cooperation among signatory states in combating terrorism and cross-border crime, especially through information exchange. By virtue of the Prüm Decision, which incorporated core elements of the Prüm Convention into its provisions, a similar decentralised framework, the 'Prüm framework', was set up.

28 In this context, it also outlines the process for automated access and comparison of DNA analysis files, fingerprint data, and vehicle registration data held in national databases, while it also details enhanced police cooperation measures like joint investigations.

29 The ECRIS FD was adopted in 2009 to streamline and organise information exchange on convictions, which led to the establishment of ECRIS by virtue of Council Decision

facilitate the exchange of information in connection to criminal convictions stored in the national criminal records databases.[30] Member States rarely used ECRIS for third country nationals,[31] so, in the context of fighting serious crime and terrorism, a proposal was put forward to extend ECRIS to explicitly cover third country nationals, by setting up a separate and centralised *ECRIS-TCN* system,[32] which was finally established in 2019.[33] Lastly, the *PNR system* is the most loosely connected with criminal law in terms of the data gathered, which relates to passenger information with regard to flights. At first, the API Directive provided for the collection of such data for the purposes of improving border controls and combating illegal immigration,[34] while later the PNR Directive regulated the use of PNR data with the explicit purpose of preventing and combatting terrorism and other serious crime.[35]

2009/316/JHA. The ECRIS Directive recently amended the ECRIS FD and replaced Council Decision 2009/316/JHA.

30 See Council of the EU, 'ECRIS Non-Binding Manual for Practitioners' (2013) 9, on the proposed benefits of ECRIS.

31 In its original version, although ECRIS encompassed data on any person convicted in a Member State, and as such included data on convictions against third country nationals, Member States were reluctant to use it for obtaining information on third country nationals, due to the largely inefficient and costly process involved; Commission, 'Explanatory Memorandum of Proposal for a Regulation establishing a centralised system for the identification of Member States holding conviction information on third country nationals and stateless persons (TCN) to supplement and support the European Criminal Records Information System (ECRIS TCN system) and amending Regulation (EU) No 1077/2011' COM (2017) 344, 2.

32 The need to combat terrorism was often stated as the impetus for the relevant talks that began in 2015, especially after the deadly terrorist attacks of November 2015 in Paris; Conclusions of the Council on enhancing the criminal justice response to radicalisation leading to terrorism and violent extremism, 20 November 2015, 14419/15 and Conclusions of the European Council meeting of 17 and 18 December 2015, EUCO 28/15. A relevant objective was included in the European Agenda on Security—COM (2015) 185, 7. After a lengthy process, on 29.6.2017 a Proposal for a Regulation was put forward to establish a separate, centralised ECRIS-TCN as a system that focuses on third country nationals.

33 The Regulation was adopted on 17.4.2019.

34 Council Directive 2004/82/EC of 29 April 2004 on the obligation of carriers to communicate passenger data [2004] OJ L 261/24 (*API Directive*) established an obligation for air carriers to submit to borders control authorities advanced passenger data, such as names, dates of birth and nationalities, travel documents details and journey details, for the aim of improving border controls and combating illegal immigration; see API Directive art 3(2).

35 The PNR Directive mandated air carriers to transfer to Member States the PNR data they already collect with regard to extra-EU flights (ie those destined to depart from a Member State and land in a third country or vice versa—see PNR Directive arts 1 and 3), with a possibility for Member States to extend that obligation to intra-EU flights as well (art 2). See PNR Directive Annex I as to what data air carriers collect as PNR data. This data can be

1.2 Centralised Systems

Centralised EU information systems are more loosely connected with criminal law aims than the decentralised ones, with the exception of the Europol database and the new ECRIS-TCN. *Europol*[36] centrally collects data related to criminal offences[37] in the context of its mandate to coordinate action against organised crime, terrorism and other serious crime across Member States, while data sharing is achieved through the Europol Information System (EIS)[38] and the Secure Information Exchange Network Application (SIENA).[39] The newly established *ECRIS-TCN* also aims to facilitate the exchange of conviction information on third-country nationals by identifying Member States that hold relevant information and enabling its exchange through ECRIS.[40] By contrast, *SIS*,[41] which consists of a central information system and connected national

shared with other competent national authorities, other Member States, or Europol (art 4), or even transferred to third countries under certain conditions (art 11).

36 Europol was established in the framework of police cooperation by the Convention based on Article K.3 of the TEU (Europol Convention) [1995] OJ C 316/2, later replaced by Council Decision 2009/371/JHA of 6 April 2009 [2009] OJ L 121/37, and subsequently by the Europol Regulation, as the leading EU agency coordinating action against combating organised crime, terrorism and other serious crime. Among its main tasks is to engage in data collection and support Member States in data sharing (Europol Regulation art 4).

37 This includes personal data of persons convicted or suspected of having committed offences falling under its mandate (Europol Regulation art 18). See also arts 17 on sources of information, 18–19 on purposes of processing data, 20–21 and 52 on access by Member States, Europol and other EU agencies to the information stored by Europol, as well as Annex II on the types of data collected, and Annex I for the crimes that fall under Europol's mandate.

38 EIS is a central database launched in 2005, which holds the information collected by Europol. For more information, see <www.europol.europa.eu/activities-services/services-support/information-exchange/europol-information-system> accessed 2 February 2020.

39 SIENA is a secure exchange platform launched in 2009. For more information, see <www.europol.europa.eu/activities-services/services-support/information-exchange/secure-information-exchange-network-application-siena> accessed 2 February 2020.

40 See ECRIS-TCN Regulation preamble para 10 (indicatively).

41 First set up in the context of the Schengen acquis that was incorporated into EU law through the Treaty of Amsterdam, SIS is a central system that serves both the aim of promoting security and of facilitating border controls; see 'Protocol integrating the Schengen acquis into the framework of the EU' [1997] OJ C 340/93. The second-generation SIS II became operational in April 2013 (see Commission, Press Release, IP/13/309) and its framework was recently updated by Regulation (EU) 2018/1861 of 28 November 2018 on the establishment, operation and use of the Schengen Information System (SIS) in the field of border checks, and amending the Convention implementing the Schengen Agreement, and amending and repealing Regulation (EC) No 1987/2006 [2018] OJ L 312/14,

systems with secure communication channels, serves the dual purpose of promoting security and facilitating border controls.[42] In a recent development, the new SIS Regulation, aspiring to establish 'a Union information system',[43] has set the foundations to immensely reinforce the aspects of the system that relate to criminal law, especially (but also indicatively) by introducing functions that aim to complement the Prüm mechanism[44] and by adjusting the alerts concerning European arrest warrants directly in line with the provisions of the respective EU legislative act, so as to increase the latter's effectiveness.[45] The *Eurodac database* was also set up[46] mainly in order to aid in the implementation of the Dublin Regulation,[47] which governs jurisdiction on asylum applications, but was later extended to allow access by designated authorities and Europol under certain conditions, for the

and the SIS Regulation in the field of police and judicial cooperation, introducing changes that will for the most part come into effect three years after the full application of the new Regulations.

42 These secure communication channels that include the Supplementary Information Request at National Entries (SIRENE) network. The main aim of SIS II, which is still operational until the new SIS Regulation comes into force, is to enhance security within the area of freedom, security and justice [Regulation (EC) 1987/2006 art 1] by enabling the sharing of data sets (called 'alerts' under SIS II). The SIS II Decision has further extended access to SIS II by law enforcement authorities, including national criminal justice judicial authorities (art 40), Europol (art 41) and Eurojust (art 42), for the purpose of police and judicial cooperation in criminal matters (art 2).

43 SIS Regulation preamble para 71.

44 SIS Regulation preamble para 21.

45 SIS Regulation preamble paras 28, 41–42.

46 The Eurodac system was established by virtue of the Eurodac Regulation—see art 1(1). Eurodac is a central system which stores and compares fingerprints and background data of applicants for international protection (Eurodac Regulation arts 9ff) and persons apprehended while irregularly crossing borders (arts 14ff) who are over 14 years old. On 4.5.2016 a Proposal for a Regulation was put forward to extend Eurodac [COM (2016) 272; on its reasoning and links to the migrant crisis, see its Explanatory Memorandum], in order to inter alia include persons who are not international protection applicants, thus serving wider immigration control purposes, as well as enable sharing data with third countries for return purposes [art 38 COM (2016) 272].

47 Regulation (EU) No 604/2013 of 26 June 2013 establishing the criteria and mechanisms for determining the Member State responsible for examining an application for international protection lodged in one of the Member States by a third-country national or a stateless person [2013] OJ L 180/31 (*Dublin Regulation*).

purposes of combating terrorism and serious crime.[48] Similarly, *VIS*,[49] *EES*[50] and *ETIAS*[51] were primarily established in order to facilitate and reinforce the management of external borders with the aim of enhancing security, but their scope was also extended to include the secondary purpose of combating terrorism and other serious crime by allowing access to designated national authorities and Europol.[52]

---

48 Eurodac Regulation arts 5, 6, 7 and 19ff.

49 By virtue of Council Decision 2004/512/EC the VIS was established, a centralised information system, with connected national interfaces in each Member State, that includes information on applications for short-term visas and the subsequent decisions made by Member States. By virtue of the VIS Decision, conditional access to VIS was extended to designated authorities and Europol for combating terrorism and other serious crime, while Regulation (EC) 767/2008 of 9 July 2008 concerning the VIS and the exchange of data between Member States on short-stay visas (*VIS Regulation*) [2008] OJ L 218/60 further defined its scope and functions. VIS became operational in October 2011, along with a Biometric Matching System that provided fingerprint matching services to VIS [see Commission, 'Report from the Commission to the European Parliament and the Council on the development of the VIS in 2011' COM (2012) 376].

50 The EES was established by virtue of the EES Regulation and is set to become operational by 2020. It consists of a central system with national interfaces that will gather data on short-term stays of third country nationals (with exceptions—EES Regulation art 2), including biometric data and information on authorised stays, while it will also issue alerts on overstayers (art 12). EES data can be made available to designated authorities and Europol for combating terrorism and serious crime [art 1(2)], including data that pertains to suspects, perpetrators, and victims of crimes [arts 6(2), 32 and 33]. On 16.5.2018, a new Proposal for a Regulation was put forward to amend the EES Regulation, while also further expanding the scope of VIS to cover long-stay visas and residence permits—see COM (2018) 302.

51 Set to become operational by 2021, the new ETIAS was introduced by virtue of the ETIAS Regulation. ETIAS applies to third country nationals who are exempt from the requirement to have a visa (ETIAS Regulation art 2) and can be consulted by designated authorities and Europol for the purposes of combating terrorism and serious crime [art 1(1)]. It consists of a Central ETIAS Information System that connects to national interfaces and holds personal data and background information on applicants (art 6; also see arts 19f and 17), an ETIAS Central Unit within the European Border and Coast Guard Agency (art 7), and designated ETIAS National Units (art 8). The ETIAS Central System will also connect to SIS information (art 23) and encompass a 'watchlist' on persons who are suspected of terrorism or other serious crimes (art 34).

52 Regarding SIS II, VIS, EES and ETIAS see also Commission, 'Proposal for a Regulation establishing the conditions for accessing other EU information systems for ETIAS purposes and amending Regulation (EU) 2018/1240, Regulation (EC) No 767/2008, Regulation (EU) 2017/2226 and Regulation (EU) 2018/1861' COM (2019) 4.

2 *Systematic Review of Elements Significant from a Criminal Law Perspective*

It is a primary objective of this paper to explore those elements within each system that are particularly important *from a criminal law perspective*. In order to enable a comprehensive understanding of this dimension of data collection and exchange within the area of freedom, security and justice, and to set a concrete foundation for its critical evaluation to follow, these specific elements are identified in the various systems and presented in two key *categories*: the *types* of data collected and the conditions to *access* this data for law enforcement purposes.

2.1 Types of Personal Data Collected

The *types* of personal data collected, stored in and exchanged through the systems are unquestionably relevant to criminal law, either due to their nature (criminal convictions, arrest warrants etc.) or because law enforcement authorities are granted access to them (names, fingerprints, facial images etc.) for the purpose of preventing and combating crime. Thus, defining the types of data processed in the context of information sharing is a crucial condition for establishing the latter's *scope* and subsequently evaluating its *impact*.

Against this background, a decisive distinction concerns the *subjects* of the data and depends on their *nationality*, given that some systems do not involve EU citizens and focus especially on third country nationals. Such a division appears to be reasonable at the EU level, given that the abolition of the internal border controls and the evolution of the free movement of persons within the territory of the Member States have put emphasis on safeguarding the external borders of the EU; moreover, in recent years and in view of the current immigration crisis, the link between security and immigration management has been stressed. The following overview corresponds to this divergent approach,[53] which, interestingly, at the same time reveals that information sharing for security reasons concerns EU citizens perhaps more than one might guess.[54]

53 This does not mean that the EU excludes third country nationals from the principle of equality (or other EU rights and principles); see indicatively the discussions in view of establishing ECRIS-TCN as a centralised system contrary to ECRIS being decentralised [COM (2017) 344, 8: 'These stakeholders have also pointed out that introducing a TCN-specific system that would treat TCN differently from EU nationals is possible from the point of view of the principle of equality, to the extent that it respects the essence of this principle and is objectively justified as necessary and proportional'].

54 Apart from concerns that relate to rights and principles applying within criminal proceedings (which are primarily addressed in this research) as well as privacy and data

2.1.1 *Types of Data Regarding EU Citizens*

Information concerning EU citizens *mainly* involves the following types of data:

a Information on Convictions

Information on convictions is principally collected and shared within the context of *ECRIS*; thus, the storage of the data is *decentralised*[55] and definitely concerns *EU citizens*. The *scope* of the data covered is actually rather *broad*.[56] Nonetheless, the sharing of this *sensitive* information is quite *drastic*, given that, when a national of a Member State is convicted in the territory of another Member State, the relevant data must be *immediately transmitted* to the Member State of the convicted person's nationality.[57] Furthermore, the latter shares upon request information on the conviction with other Member States[58] or third countries[59] for the purposes of criminal proceedings or even other purposes (e.g. pre-employment screenings). These functions are of great significance, especially considering that, within the legal order of each Member State, past convictions registered (under non-harmonised conditions) in criminal records affect the course of criminal proceedings *in several ways* (e.g. a previous conviction can influence the decision on pre-trial detention, the

protection concerns (also examined), there is also the view that the EU's data collection activity for security purposes challenges EU free movement of persons and, thus, EU citizenship (Valsamis Mitsilegas, 'European Criminal Law and the Dangerous Citizen' [2018] Maastricht Journal of European and Comparative Law 733, 747), and the very relationship between the individual and the State (Valsamis Mitsilegas, 'The Transformation of Privacy in an Era of Pre-emptive Surveillance' [2015] Tilburg Law Review 35, 50f).

55 It remains decentralised even after the amendment by the ECRIS Directive [see current ECRIS FD art 11a(1)].

56 It comprises '*obligatory information*' on the convicted person (= full name, date and place of birth, gender, nationality and previous name), on the nature (= date of conviction, name of the court, date on which the decision became final) and content of the conviction (= the sentence, supplementary penalties, security measures and any decisions modifying the enforcement of the sentence) and on the offence that led to it (= date and name or legal classification of the offence, the applicable legal provisions); '*optional information*' (= the place of the offence, the convicted person's parents' names, the reference number of the conviction and disqualifications arising from the conviction), if such are entered in the criminal record; '*additional information*' (= the convicted person's fingerprints, identity number, or the type and number of his/her identification document, facial image and, if applicable, alias name and/or pseudonym), if they are available to the competent authority; and any other information concerning the conviction entered in criminal records by a Member State [ECRIS FD art 11(1)].

57 ECRIS FD arts 4(2),(3) and 11(1).

58 See the varying obligations and possibilities of the Member States, depending on the exact content of the request, in ECRIS FD arts 7(1),(2),(4) and 11(2).

59 ECRIS FD art 7(3),(5).

decision on the type and extent of a sentence or the decision on bail); what is more, the effects on criminal proceedings *varies per Member State* (i.e. the examples given just above come from different legal orders).[60] Against this background, one may agree that the exchange of this type of data contributes to the *equal treatment between EU citizens*, in the sense that it does not seem justified for a person convicted in the past to be treated as a first-time offender if he or she chooses to commit a new criminal offence in another Member State, while another person with the same previous conviction will be treated as re-offending if he or she chooses to commit a new criminal offence in the Member State where the first conviction was handed down. Yet, since past convictions have different effects in each Member State, one might ask whether sharing information about them really serves equal treatment. In addition, obviously a person needs to have knowledge of all the national rules affected by past convictions in order to fully predict the consequences of his or her actions in another Member State, as it is clear that a single conviction registered in a national criminal record in one Member State can be linked to any relevant rule that takes a conviction into account in any other Member State.

Information related to convictions is also stored at a *central* level by *Europol* for the various purposes it pursues.[61] In total, collecting information on past

60 See the different functions of past convictions in the Member States in Commission, 'Report on the implementation by the Member States of Framework Decision 2008/675/JHA' COM (2014) 312; reference is made to the pre-trial stage [pre-trial detention; bail; principle of opportunity (= 'the discretionary power of a public prosecutor to pursue investigations into a case or halt procedures')], the trial stage (type, level and extent of a sentence/sanction; degree of guilt; conditional sentences; alternative measures to ensure the presence of the accused at court; legal classification of the offence; recidivism), and the stage of executing the conviction (probation; conditional early release; suspension of a sentence or custodial measure; deciding whether the convicted is to be placed in a high security unit or a facility for notorious recidivists; commuting a life sentence into a fixed term imprisonment). What is more, each one of the issues affected may present specific challenges; indicatively on the challenges *recidivism poses on the presumption of innocence* see Marta Muñoz de Morales Romero, 'The taking account of EU previous sanctions in joint/accumulated punishment: the Spanish case' [2018] EuCLR 244; Josh Bowers, 'Punishing the innocent' [2008] University of Pennsylvania Law Review 1117; Panagiotis Vogiatzis, The presumption of innocence (Article 6 para 2 ECHR) [in Greek] in Linos-Alexandros Sisilianos (series dir) *European Convention on Human Rights, Article Commentary* [in Greek] (2nd edn, Nomiki Bibiliothiki 2017) 301; Stefan Trechsel, *Human Rights in Criminal Proceedings* (Oxford 2005) 89; Vasilis Tzemos, *The Charter of Fundamental Rights of the EU* [in Greek] (Nomiki Bibliothiki 2015) 535ff.

61 Europol Regulation art 18. The collection of data related to convictions is possible for the purpose of *cross-checking* with regard to convictions that concern a criminal offence falling under Europol's competence [see the lengthy list of these offences in Europol Regulation Annex I and Anna Fiodorova, *Information Exchange and EU Law Enforcement*

convictions has a different function within Europol's framework, since it aims at supporting *suspicion* of a person's possible connection to a criminal offence. Assessing how dangerous a person potentially is based on past convictions may not be an unreasonable approach, however, in the case of Europol it becomes a problematic one, due to expanding the scope of the notion of 'suspicion' (which includes committing offences in the *future*) to a wide range of people loosely (or even not at all) linked to any criminal activity.[62]

The significance of previous convictions in assessing future dangers is evident within the *Prüm framework* as well, where personal data (without other clarifications, just the condition that 'the supply of such data is permitted under the supplying Member State's national law') is requested or immediately exchanged 'if any final convictions or other circumstances give reason to believe that the data subjects will commit criminal offences' during 'major events with a cross-border dimension' or 'pose a threat to public order and security'.[63]

b DNA Data

According to the *Prüm* Decision, all Member States are called to open and keep *DNA analysis files* for the investigation of criminal offences.[64] As a result, the

(1st edn, Routledge 2018) 157 for the development of Europol's competences] and it may be accompanied by relevant information [criminal offences, alleged criminal offences and when, where and how they were (allegedly) committed; means which were or which may have been used to commit those criminal offences, including information concerning legal persons; departments handling the case and their filing references; suspected membership of a criminal organisation—Europol Regulation Annex II.A(3)(e)]. Previous convictions may also be collected *for the purpose of analyses of a strategic or thematic nature, for the purpose of operational analyses or for the purpose of facilitating the exchange of information*, accompanied with expanded data on the person's criminal conduct [suspected involvement in criminal activities; modi operandi; means which were or may be used to prepare and/or commit crimes; membership of criminal groups/organisations and position in the group/organisation; role in the criminal organisation; geographical range of criminal activities; material gathered in the course of an investigation, such as video and photographic images—Europol Regulation Annex II.B(2)(j)(i)].

62 The collection of personal data concerns persons who are suspected of having committed or participated in such a criminal offence, or who have been convicted of one, or for whom there are reasonable grounds to believe that they *will commit* one in the future, or *who have regular or sporadic contacts with one of the abovementioned persons* (Europol Regulation Annex II).

63 Prüm Decision art 14(1).

64 Prüm Decision art 2. See Fiodorova 187–208; Daniela Kietz and Andreas Maurer, *From Schengen to Prüm. Deeper Integration through Enhanced Cooperation or Signs of Fragmentation in the EU?* (SWP Comments 2017) <www.swp-berlin.org/fileadmin/contents/products/comments/Com15_06_Ktz_Mrr_Ks.pdf> accessed on 1 February 2020; Elspeth Guild, *Merging Security from Two-Level Game: Inserting the Treaty of Prüm into EU law?*

storage of the relevant data is *decentralised*; however, in what is the most controversial version of decentralised information collection and sharing in the EU, the competent authorities within each Member State can *automatically* search the database of any other Member State.[65] In addition, when requested, Member States are *obliged* to provide legal assistance to other Member States in the framework of criminal proceedings, by obtaining and supplying DNA profiles of individuals present in their territory. DNA profiles are also collected as means of identification at a *central* level by *Europol*, in a similar context and, most importantly in terms of a person's rights, for the same categories of persons as information on convictions presented just above.[66] Lastly, it is worth noting that, under the new SIS Regulation, it should become possible to enter DNA data *into SIS*, thus *centrally*, for specific categories of missing persons.[67] Apart from the significance of the very fact that SIS will be able to collect such data, hence making a future expansion of the scope of this collection easier, 'missing persons' are further defined in a way that appears to affect criminal law [: as persons 'who need to be placed under protection' either for their own protection or *so as to prevent a threat to public order or public security* (whereas the respective phrase in the SIS II Decision is 'to prevent threats')].[68]

c Fingerprints, Palm Prints and Photographs

Within the Prüm framework, Member States are called to 'ensure the availability' of reference data in the national automated *fingerprint* identification systems;[69] consequently, every competent national authority must have *access* to this reference data *in any Member State*, so as to perform searches by comparing dactyloscopic data for the prevention and investigation of criminal offences.[70] The collection and sharing of data concerning fingerprints is conducted in the same manner as regarding DNA profiles by *Europol*,[71] while fingerprints may be exchanged through *ECRIS* too, as part of 'additional

(CEPS 2007); Elspeth Guild and Florian Geyer, *Getting local: Schengen, Prüm and the dancing procession of Echternach; Three paces forward and two back for EU police and judicial cooperation* (CEPS 2006); Lampros Margaritis and Elisavet Kastanidou (eds), *DNA Analysis in criminal trial* [*DNA analysis*] [in Greek] (Nomiki Bibliothiki 2014); Maria Kaiafa-Gbandi and others, *DNA analysis and court practice* [in Greek] (Sakkoulas 2014).

65 Prüm Decision art 3.

66 Europol Regulation art 18 and Annex II.A(2)(g) and B(2)(c)(v).

67 SIS Regulation art 42(3) and preamble para 26.

68 SIS Regulation art 32(1)(a).

69 Prüm Decision art 8(1).

70 Prüm Decision art 9.

71 Europol Regulation art 18 and Annex II.A(2)(g) and B(2)(c)(v).

information' attached to a conviction.[72] Furthermore, *SIS* contains fingerprint data[73] regarding *alerts* issued on persons to be used along with *photographs* for the *confirmation* of the identity (i.e. not as primary means of identification) of a person located using SIS 'alphanumerical data'.[74] SIS data is extremely important from a criminal law perspective, since it is linked to *alerts* entailing corresponding *duties* for the authorities to *act* upon, most notably for the purpose of *executing arrest warrants*[75] or for the purpose of *communicating the place of residence of persons involved in criminal proceedings*;[76] on the other hand, there are also alerts of clear *preventive* nature regarding even offences assumed to be committed in the future and preventing threats to public security.[77] Presently, the new SIS Regulation aims to intensely enhance the use of dactyloscopic data (which will include fingerprints *and palm prints*), most importantly by introducing provisions on the *automated fingerprint identification service*,[78] which has already been launched by the eu-LISA Internal Security Systems Sector in 2018, enabling 'the identification of a person from his/her fingerprints alone'.[79] What is extremely interesting from a criminal law perspective is that, according to the SIS Regulation, the objective of the automated fingerprint identification service is to *complement 'the Prüm mechanism* on mutual cross-border online access' to national DNA databases and national fingerprint identification systems, with a view to identifying unknown perpetrators of a serious crime or of an act of terrorism.[80] Therefore, SIS, a centralised information system, is stepping much deeper into law enforcement activity, while the Prüm framework is complemented in terms of effectiveness instead of improved in terms of guarantees.

---

72 ECRIS FD art 11(1)(c).

73 SIS II Decision art 20.

74 That is data represented by letters, digits, etc. (eg their name); SIS II Decision art 22.

75 Either European arrest warrants or other types of arrest warrants based on EU agreements with third countries; SIS II Decision arts 3(2) and 26–31.

76 That is witnesses, persons (to be) summoned to appear before judicial authorities, persons to be served a criminal judgment or documents related to their prosecution, or persons to be summoned in order to serve a penalty involving deprivation of liberty; SIS II Decision art 34.

77 These alerts concern *discreet or specific checks*, conducted when there is *'clear indication' that a person intends to commit or is committing* a serious criminal offence, or *an 'overall assessment' of a person gives reason to suppose that he/she will commit serious criminal offences in the future*; SIS II Decision art 36.

78 See SIS Regulation art 43(2) and SIS II Decision art 22(3).

79 See information in <www.eulisa.europa.eu/Newsroom/PressRelease/Pages/eu-LISA-successfully-launches-SIS-II-AFIS-Phase-One.aspx> accessed 1 February 2020.

80 See most notably SIS Regulation preamble para 23.

d [Other] Identification Data

Other identification data[81] is collected by different systems with varying content. At a *central* level, it is stored for all the categories of the persons involved in the data collection carried out by *Europol*,[82] and also in SIS in relation to the alerts it contains.[83] At a *decentralised* level, it is transmitted and exchanged through ECRIS;[84] it is collected by the Member States as provided by air carriers in the context of the *PNR* Directive;[85] and it may be supplied even immediately by the Member States (in compliance with their national law) through

81 That is in the form of alphanumerical representation (name, surname, place of residence etc.) as just mentioned above.

82 For the purpose of *cross-checking*: surname, maiden name, given names and any alias or assumed name; date and place of birth; nationality; sex; place of residence, profession and whereabouts of the person concerned; social security numbers, driving licences, identification documents and passport data [Europol Regulation Annex II.A(2)]. For the *other purposes pursued by Europol*: (personal details:) present and former surnames, present and former forenames, maiden name, father's name (where necessary for the purpose of identification), mother's name (where necessary for the purpose of identification), sex, date of birth, place of birth, nationality, marital status, alias, nickname, assumed or false name, present and former residence and/or domicile; (physical description:) physical description, distinguishing features (marks/scars/tattoos etc.); (means of identification:) identity documents/driving licence, national identity card/passport numbers, national identification number/social security number, if applicable, other information on appearance (apart from visual images), voice profile, blood group, dental information [Europol Regulation Annex II.B(2)].

83 Surname and forename, name at birth and previously used names and any aliases; any specific, objective, physical characteristics not subject to change; place and date of birth; sex; nationality—Regulation (EC) 1987/2006 art 20(2) [see also art 36(3) therein]. Based on SIS Regulation art 20(2), the following identification data will be added: category/country of issue/the number/the date of issue of the person's identification documents [see also art 62(3) therein].

84 As part of obligatory information [full name, date of birth, place of birth (town and State), gender, nationality and—if applicable—previous name—ECRIS FD art 11(1)(a)(i)]; as part of optional information [the convicted person's parents' names—ECRIS FD art 11(1)(b)(i)]; as part of additional information [the convicted person's identity number, or the type and number of the person's identification document; if applicable, pseudonym and/or alias name—ECRIS FD art 11(1)(c)(i),(iii)].

85 Name, address and contact information (telephone number, e-mail address), the API data (type, number, country of issuance and expiry date of any identity document, nationality, family name, given name, gender, date of birth); in relation to minors, name and gender of the minor, age, language(s) spoken, name and contact details of guardian on departure and relationship to the minor, name and contact details of guardian on arrival and relationship to the minor—PNR Directive Annex I.

the Prüm framework,[86] when particular circumstances give reason to believe that the data subjects *will* commit terrorist offences.

e Information Regarding Air Travel

Apart from information relating to the identity of a person, the *PNR Directive*, also an advanced framework of *decentralised* data collection and exchange, principally involves information regarding air travel.[87] Although information of a somewhat similar type was already collected and transmitted to the authorities *when requested* on the basis of the API Directive, the special significance of the PNR Directive lies in the fact that the data collected by air carriers for commercial reasons are *all transferred* to the corresponding national unit *for storage*, to be used for the purpose of 'preventing, detecting, investigating and prosecuting terrorist offences and serious crime'. In spite of this specific purpose, though, PNR data is not limited to persons considered as suspects; by the Directive's own admission 'assessment of PNR data allows identification of persons who were *unsuspected* of involvement in terrorist offences or serious crime *prior to such an assessment* and who should be subject to further examination by the competent authorities'.[88] However, the conditions under which it is possible to treat every person travelling as a potential suspect with regard to all the said offences (not even just to offences where travelling is independently criminalised, namely terrorist offences[89] or sexual offences against children[90]—which of course are themselves extremely controversial) is an issue to further explore.

---

86 Surname, first names, date and place of birth (and a description of the circumstances giving rise to the belief that a terrorist offence will be committed); Prüm Decision art 16.

87 According to Annex I of the PNR Directive, passenger name record data as far as collected by air carriers also includes: PNR record locator, date of reservation/issue of ticket, date(s) of intended travel, all forms of payment information, complete travel itinerary, frequent flyer information, travel agency/travel agent, travel status of passenger, split/divided PNR information, general remarks (including all available information on unaccompanied minors under 18 years), ticketing field information, seat number and other seat information, code share information, all baggage information, number and other names of travellers on the PNR, other API data collected (airline, flight number, departure date, arrival date, departure port, arrival port, departure time and arrival time) and all historical changes to the information listed above.

88 PNR Directive preamble para 7.

89 Directive (EU) 2017/541 art 9.

90 Sex tourism is not explicitly criminalised under Directive 2011/93/EU, however, it is covered by its scope: firstly, the attempt to contact the child falls within the definition of solicitation (art 6); secondly, *art 21 criminalises the organising and advertising for child sex tourism*; thirdly, it is mentioned in the Directive's preamble para 29 that 'Member States should foster open dialogue and communication with countries outside the Union

f Other Types of Data Collected by Europol

Finally, it is essential to note that *Europol* collects not only all the types of data presented above (with the exception of PNR data), but actually a lot more and for a wide range of people. Most importantly, the categories of the persons involved are up to a great degree formed under the criterion of detecting weak or questionable links (not to criminal offences but) to *persons suspected* to be somehow connected to criminal activity. Indicatively, Europol may store ***data on 'occupation and skills'***,[91] ***'behavioural data'***[92] or ***economic and financial information***[93] for a person for whom there are reasonable grounds to believe that he or she *will commit* a criminal offence; *the same types of data can even be stored for a person in sporadic contact with the suspect*, if there is sufficient reason to believe that in this way *information on the suspect can be gained* (not on the subject of the data nor for a criminal offence; thus the subject of the data is just used in the process of obtaining information on the suspect).[94] Bearing in mind that there are more categories of data exclusively linked to specific categories of persons (to victims and possible victims, witnesses and possible witnesses, informers and possible informers), Europol's database is itself a major issue as regards respecting the right to privacy, but also in connection to the other reasons that have dictated the decentralised character of storing the same information by national authorities in the Member States, generating

---

in order to be able to prosecute perpetrators, under the relevant national legislation, who travel outside the Union borders for the purposes of child sex tourism'. In 2007, the Greek legislator criminalised types of conduct relating to child sex tourism, including participating in respective travelling (see former art 323B, currently art 348(2) of the Greek Criminal Code) in ratifying the UN 'Optional Protocol to the Convention on the Rights of the Child on the sale of children, child prostitution and child pornography' of 25 May 2000.

91 It includes present employment and occupation, former employment and occupation, education (school/university/professional), qualifications, skills and other fields of knowledge (language/other)—Europol Regulation Annex II.B(2)(d).

92 It includes lifestyle (such as living above means) and routine, movements, places frequented, weapons and other dangerous instrument, danger rating, specific risks such as escape probability, use of double agents, connections with law enforcement personnel, criminal-related traits and profiles, drug abuse—Europol Regulation Annex II.B(2)(f).

93 It includes financial data (bank accounts and codes, credit cards, etc.), cash assets, shareholdings and other assets, property data, links with companies, bank and credit contacts, tax position, other information revealing a person's management of his/her financial affairs—Europol Regulation Annex II.B(2)(e).

94 Europol processes several other categories of data as well [contacts and associates, means of communication used, means of transport used, information on legal persons associated with certain categories of data, references to other information systems in which information on the person is stored (Europol, police/customs agencies, other enforcement agencies, international organisations, public entities, private entities)—Europol Regulation Annex II.B(2)].

more concern when considered against sharing information with third countries or interacting with other EU information systems.[95]

2.1.2 *Types of Data Regarding TCNs*

All the rules on the types of data cited in the previous section apply equally to third country nationals;[96] however, additional rules apply solely to them, especially since information systems designed for external borders control and for managing migration to the EU also serve law enforcement purposes.

In this regard, it should be noted that ***fingerprints***,[97] ***photographs***[98] and ***alphanumerical identity data***[99] collected is accessible for the purpose of preventing and combating crime as well. This is an *important input of data* for the competent authorities in the Member States and for EU agencies, especially Europol. And although this vast collection of information appears to be justified (unlike in the case of PNR) in view of the primary, or at least parallel, objective of controlling the EU's external borders, it is necessary, insofar as it does not just entail e.g. entry denials, but it is also linked to the administration of criminal justice within the EU, to determine whether it is justified to its *full* extent or whether it leads to a blanket collection of data of third country nationals by the EU.

Finally, a major development has occurred with the adoption of the ECRIS-TCN Regulation, based on which *fingerprints*,[100] *facial images*[101] and *alphanumerical identity data*[102] of every third-country national convicted in an EU Member State will be at a central level, under varying conditions, available to the competent authorities to use to identify the Member State holding information on a past conviction. Accessing the ECRIS-TCN will be possible

95 See Fiodorova 135 for criticism on functions of Europol in the field of information sharing, indicatively regarding Europol Regulation art 18(7), by which what was added in flexibility was taken away in legal certainty. For more on Europol, see inter alia Maria Kaiafa-Gbandi, 'Coordinating organs in the fight against organised crime in the EU: From Police (Europol) to judicial (Eurojust) cooperation' [in Greek] [2003] Poiniki Dikaiosyni 165; Sabine Gless, 'Europol' in *Research Handbook* 457–479; Gaetano De Amicis and Roberto E. Kostoris, 'Vertical Cooperation' in *Handbook criminal procedure* 211ff.

96 Until recently the ECRIS data was excluded; this has changed based on the provisions introduced in the ECRIS FD by the recent ECRIS Directive [eg see the new provisions in arts 2(e), 4(1), 6(3a), 7(4a)].

97 VIS Regulation art 5; Eurodac Regulation arts 11 and 14; EES Regulation arts 17–18.

98 VIS Regulation art 5; EES Regulation arts 15, 17–18.

99 VIS Regulation art 5; Eurodac Regulation arts 11 and 14 (not including information related to name); EES Regulation arts 16–18; ETIAS Regulation art 17.

100 ECRIS-TCN Regulation art 5(b).

101 ECRIS-TCN Regulation art 6.

102 ECRIS-TCN Regulation art 5(a).

for the purposes of criminal proceedings against the third country national involved, but also for an important number of other purposes.[103] Although convictions themselves will be stored in the *national* criminal records, this is a significant first step towards a *centralised function* concerning *principally criminal law data* for *criminal law purposes* in the context of *judicial* cooperation. Furthermore, this is a key evolution also in terms of its effect on EU citizens, not only because ECRIS has long been holding information on EU citizens, but also because the centralised operation of ECRIS-TCN *already* affects them: under article 7(4) of the ECRIS-TCN Regulation 'the competent authorities may also query ECRIS-TCN to verify whether, in respect of a citizen of the Union, any Member State holds criminal records information concerning this person as a third-country national'.

2.2 Access to Data for Law Enforcement Purposes

The conditions on *accessing* the data stored are of central importance for criminal law, because it is the act of *processing* the data that eventually materialises any risks set by collecting it. In the cases of the decentralised systems (ECRIS, the Prüm framework, the PNR data) and the Europol data, it has already been mentioned that data is mainly processed by a competent authority or the agency collecting it and either exchanged (ECRIS, PNR) or automatically searched (Prüm) by authorities of other Member States. However, things are different as far as the systems collecting information for external borders control are concerned. These systems set specific *prerequisites* for the competent authorities to access the data stored *for law enforcement purposes*, which are of major significance from a fundamental rights and criminal law perspective, because they constitute (or should constitute) a *barrier preventing possible abuse* and a stage where authorities are required to provide *reasoned arguments regarding the connection between a person and a criminal offence*.

Indeed, in order to avoid the *unnecessary or regular* use of 'immigration data' for law enforcement purposes, all the relevant systems (VIS, Eurodac, EES and ETIAS) have established *a set of conditions* with respect to allowing such access.

Firstly, they contain a similar approach on the crucial term '*law enforcement*' (defined as 'the prevention, detection or investigation of terrorist offences or of other serious criminal offences')[104] as well as its components, namely '*terrorist*

---

103 ECRIS-TCN Regulation art 7(1): checking a person's own criminal record at his/her request, security clearance, obtaining a licence or permit, employment vetting, vetting for voluntary activities involving direct and regular contacts with children or vulnerable persons, visa, acquisition of citizenship and migration procedures, including asylum procedures, and checks in relation with public contracts and public examinations.

104 Eurodac Regulation art 2(1)(i), EES Regulation art 3, ETIAS Regulation art 3.

offences'[105] and other '*serious criminal offences*'.[106] At an abstract level, using the definition of criminal offences to delineate the powers of an authority entails *clarity*, while evoking the need to deal with grave offences may substantially add to justifying access to information; nevertheless, both legal instruments cited are heavily burdened by the very broad scope, the unclear content and the deeply problematic provisions on the criminal offences they involve.[107]

Secondly, the assessment of the respective conditions is as a rule assigned to *two* independent authorities, where one[108] submits a *reasoned* request for access and the other one [109] *checks and verifies* that the conditions are fulfilled. This requirement appears to be so important that it largely applies to Europol too.[110] The safeguards deriving from the said procedure are weakened

105 According to EES Regulation art 3(1)(24) and ETIAS Regulation art 3(1)(15), '*terrorist offence* means an offence which corresponds or is equivalent to one of the offences referred to in Directive (EU) 2017/541' on combating terrorism [2017] OJ L 88/6; this Directive is critical for all the other systems as well, because it has repealed and replaced Framework Decision 2002/475/JHA on terrorism [VIS Decision art 2(1)(c), Eurodac Regulation art 2(1)(j)].

106 *Serious criminal offences* means the forms of crime which correspond or are equivalent to those referred to in art 2(2) of Framework Decision 2002/584/JHA of 13 June 2002 on the European arrest warrant and the surrender procedures between Member States [2002] OJ L 190/1, if punishable under national law by a custodial sentence or a detention order for a maximum period of at least three years [Eurodac Regulation art 2(1)(k), EES Regulation art 3(1)(25), ETIAS Regulation art 3(1)(16); in VIS Decision art 2(1)(d) the three year limit is not included].

107 Maria Kaiafa-Gbandi, 'Supranational delineation of criminal repression: ideological developmental axes of EU criminal law' [in Greek] [2018] Poinika Chronika, 497, 502–503; Nikolaos Paraskevopoulos, *Majorities in the Crosshairs—Terrorism and the Rule of Law* (Patakis 2003); Ioannis Manoledakis, *Global Power and Legal Culture* [in Greek] (Sakkoulas 2005); Elisavet Symeonidou-Kastanidou, *Organised Crime and Terrorism* [in Greek] (Sakkoulas 2007); Valsamis Mitsilegas, 'The Borders Paradox: The Surveillance of Movement in a Union without Internal Frontiers' in Hans Lindahl (ed), *A Right to Inclusion and Exclusion? Normative Fault Lines of the EU's Area of Freedom, Security and Justice* (Hart Publishing 2009) 54ff, who argues that combating terrorism is often used as an excuse to streamline data exchange; Dafni Lima, 'Criminalising Organised Crime on the EU Level: Understanding Crime through a Financial Aim Perspective?' in Jannemieke Ouwerkerk and other (eds), *The Future of EU Criminal Justice Policy and Practice—Legal and Criminological Perspectives* (Brill 2019) 169–180; Curtin 67–68; Kreissl 93ff.

108 The designated authority (Eurodac Regulation art 19) or the operating unit (VIS Decision art 4) or the operating unit within the designated authority (EES Regulation art 31, ETIAS Regulation art 50).

109 The verifying authority for Eurodac or the central access point for VIS, EES and ETIAS.

110 See EES Regulation art 33(4) (request by Europol designated authority/ verification by Europol central access point); ETIAS Regulation art 53(3) (request by Europol/ prior verification by a specialised unit of duly empowered Europol officials); cf. VIS Decision art 7

in '*exceptional cases of urgency*', where the need to prevent an *imminent danger* may lead to transmitting the request immediately and assessing the fulfilment of the critical conditions *afterwards*; should this *ex-post verification*[111] reveal that accessing the relevant database was *not justified*, the data acquired must be *erased*. Undoubtedly, the fact that special safeguards are added to the exception is very positive, as long as the ex-post verification maintains its exceptional character and remains unaffected by the outcome of the search.

Based on the above, the conditions assessed within the said procedure appear to be essentially *similar*, or at least comparable, in each of the legal instruments on the concerned systems. As a result, they reveal a *common concept* with regard to the attributes that accessing 'immigration data' for law enforcement purposes should bear. In particular, this common concept first of all entails that, before accessing a central system, other databases, less invasive to the rights of the subject of the data, should be searched or consulted. This *subsidiary* role of searching a central system is quite welcome, as in criminal law standards it relates to the fundamental principle that using onerous measures must not be the first choice of an authority (ultima ratio). Even so, turning to the automated search of the Prüm framework, which in essence functions like a centralised system itself, is not a mild choice,[112] especially in view of enhancing its practical operation within the last couple of years. On the other hand, the rest of the conditions have a rather clear reference to criteria examined under the principle of *proportionality*: access must be *necessary for the purpose* of the prevention, detection or investigation of offences;[113] access must be *necessary*[114] (*and proportionate*)[115] *in a specific case* (i.e. a comparison shall not be carried out as an end in itself); there must be *evidence or reasonable grounds* to consider that access will substantially contribute to

(access by a specialised unit with duly empowered Europol officials to act as the central access point/ processing of information obtained by Europol subject to the consent of the Member State which has entered that data in the VIS), Eurodac Regulation art 21 (request by Europol's designated authority/ processing of information obtained by Europol subject to the authorisation of the Member State of origin).

111 Ex-post verification must take place without delay after processing the request and include an evaluation of the reasons justifying urgency.

112 Kaiafa-Gbandi, 'Information exchange' 149.

113 Eurodac Regulation art 20(1)(a) provides a definition of the condition (it 'means that there is an overriding public security concern which makes the searching of the database proportionate'), VIS Decision art 5(1)(a), EES Regulation art 32(1)(a), ETIAS Regulation art 52(1)(a).

114 Eurodac Regulation art 20(1)(b), VIS Decision art 5(1)(b), EES Regulation art 32(1)(b), ETIAS Regulation art 52(1)(b).

115 The VIS and Eurodac provisions do not contain this reference.

the prevention, detection or investigation of the criminal offences in question ('such reasonable grounds exist in particular where there is a substantiated suspicion that the suspect, perpetrator or victim of a terrorist offence or other serious criminal offence falls in a category covered by' the founding legislative act of each system).[116] Similar conditions apply to assessing Europol's access as well.[117]

Finally, it should be added that, when it comes to SIS, its special nature to function at a central level but also rely on national files, as well as its *dual* purpose, are reflected in the provisions on access rights, which deviate significantly from what was just presented above.[118] In the same direction, the ECRIS TCN, being the first centralised system functioning within the context of judicial cooperation in the EU, provides direct access rights to the central authorities of the Member States, Eurojust, Europol and the European Public Prosecutor's Office.[119]

2.3 Brief Remarks of Significance to Criminal Law

At this point it is important to note that, first of all, while they might employ varying terminology and do so in a varying degree, the information systems examined incorporate into their framework the *fundamental data subject rights* that are enshrined in articles 15–17 and 77ff of the new General Data Protection Regulation (GDRP), namely the right *to access, to correction, to erasure and to redress.* As a result, the protection provided to the subjects of the data appears to be two-fold: on the one hand, conditions related to determining which data is collected and how, the prerequisites for authorities accessing the data for law enforcement purposes, as well as the structure of some systems itself (namely storing data at a decentralised level) aim at *preventing* abuses of personal data when using the systems; on the other hand, rights deriving directly from data protection rules may provide for protection with regard to potential abuse, or abuse that has already taken place. This comprehensive choice made

116 Eurodac Regulation art 20(1)(c); there are similar clauses in EES Regulation art 32(1)(c) and in ETIAS Regulation art 52(1)(c), but not in VIS Decision art 52(1)(c); also, the VIS and Eurodac provisions do not refer to 'evidence'.

117 Eurodac Regulation art 21, VIS Decision art 7, EES Regulation art 33, ETIAS Regulation art 53.

118 The SIS provides for direct access and the right to search its data to authorities responsible for border controls (including police authorities) *and* national *judicial* authorities in the performance of their tasks and as regulated by national law; similarly, to Europol *and Eurojust* (see SIS II Decision arts 41 and 42 respectively; and SIS Regulation arts 48 and 49).

119 See ECRIS TCN Regulation art 7.

by the EU legislator is of fundamental significance, since it goes beyond the protection of personal data as a goal in itself.

Secondly, when assessing the elements presented above against the aim of enhancing *security*, one observes that data collection and sharing indeed goes further than referring to police cooperation and directly concerns *judicial cooperation* as well. In reality, the effects of the way the EU information systems function reach the *heart* of criminal liability, in those cases where they are unavoidably connected to the *definition* of certain criminal offences. Particularly in the field of terrorism, acts such as training, travelling to commit terrorist offences, or preparing for almost any of the criminal offences included in Directive (EU) 2017/541 are construed in a way that the gathering of *reliable information* appears crucial not only in order to support suspicions about intended terrorist offences, but also in order to prove the commission of the said offences (training or preparing), since these have been elevated from preparatory acts of actual terrorist offences harming other people's legally protected interests to self-standing crimes. Therefore, in general, there are two ways the relevant data can function: either as basis for *establishing* criminal liability (when the definition of an offence is vague, not restricted to a clearly harmful act and too dependent on subjective elements, so indications based on information *are critical in initiating criminal proceedings*) or as *guarantees* (when the definition of an offence is limited to acts actually putting legally protected interests into danger, so information may only *support* verifying or disproving a person's actions and respective intention).

In view of the above, and before reflecting on the issues set and evaluating data collecting and sharing in the EU (under Part 2), it is important to review at this point an extremely decisive evolution: rendering many of these systems *interoperable* with each other.

3 *The Interoperability Regulation*

The development of EU databases and information systems was realised in a relatively fragmented way, with no initial intention or planning of connecting the systems with one another.[120] It has been argued that this has resulted to structural shortcomings and an ineffective landscape with blind spots,[121]

120 Katharina Eisele, 'Interoperability between EU information systems for security, border and migration management' (*European Parliamentary Research Service* February 2018) PE 615.649.

121 Commission, 'Frequently asked questions—Interoperability of EU information systems for security, border and migration management (Commission FAQ)' (2017) MEMO/17/5241; Commission, Amended Interoperability Proposal COM (2018) 480, 1.

which opened up a discussion about introducing *interoperability* between selected key EU information systems.[122]

Building on the Communication on Stronger and Smarter Information Systems for Borders and Security that the Commission presented in April 2016[123] and the subsequent expert group report, the Commission introduced two sister legislative Proposals, which were voted into Regulations in 2019, one on establishing a framework for interoperability between EU information systems for borders and visa [Regulation (EU) 2019/817], affecting EES, VIS, ETIAS and SIS, and one for police and judicial cooperation, asylum and migration [Regulation (EU) 2019/818, hereinafter Interoperability Regulation], which is more closely connected to criminal law and law enforcement, encompassing changes to Eurodac, SIS and ECRIS-TCN.[124]

According to the Commission, interoperability 'is the ability of information systems to exchange data and enable sharing of information';[125] it will not result in pooling all data from the underlying systems or in collecting additional categories of data (although this claim has been met with scepticism).[126]

The Interoperability Regulation aims to establish four main processes/tools for accessing data across several information systems.[127] The first of these tools is the European Search Portal (ESP) that will serve as a platform in order to search all interconnected systems simultaneously by launching a single

122 While the concept of interoperability has been on the table for a while, it has recently undergone rapid developments beginning with the Communication on Stronger and Smarter Information Systems for Borders and Security (April 2016) and the subsequent establishment of a high-level expert group in June 2016 that published its final report in May 2017.

123 COM (2016) 205.

124 The Regulations are for the most part identical in their content, intended to constitute two versions of the same underlying document, even though they differ in their scope and in the content of some of their provisions accordingly. Obviously, the Regulation on police and judicial cooperation, asylum and migration (Interoperability Regulation) is more closely connected to the scope of this paper. This section builds on the paper 'Combating Crime in the Digital Age: New Technologies in the Service of Security and Challenges for Personal Data Protection—A Critical Review of the Proposed EU Interoperability Framework for Police and Judicial Cooperation, Asylum and Migration' presented by Athina Giannakoula and Dafni Lima at the IV CINETS Conference 2018 (5–6 October 2018, Queen Mary University of London).

125 Commission FAQ.

126 See primarily European Data Protection Supervisor (EDPS), 'Opinion 4/2018 on the Proposals for two Regulations establishing a framework for interoperability between EU large-scale information systems' (16 April 2018) (*EDPS*).

127 These will be developed and managed by eu-LISA, the European Agency for the operational management of large-scale IT Systems in the area of freedom, security and justice.

query, instead of searching each individual system separately.[128] Secondly, a Shared Biometric Matching Service (BMS) will be established, which will centrally store templates of biometric data (facial images and fingerprints)[129] and encompass a search engine that will allow users to search and cross-match this data, detecting multiple biometric entries. The same principle underlies the establishment of a Common Identity Repository (CIR), which is envisioned as 'a shared container of identity data, travel document data and biometric data'[130] and which will create a personal file on each individual person recorded under Eurodac, ECRIS-TCN, EES, VIS, and ETIAS, and thus streamline identification of non-EU citizens by law enforcement authorities.[131] Finally, the Multiple Identity Detector (MID) is specifically set up to detect multiple or fraudulent identities, by creating, storing and labelling links on data contained in the CIR and SIS.[132] The Commission is also proposing three additional measures for increased efficiency, namely a central repository for reporting and statistics (CRRS),[133] the adoption of the Universal Message Format (UMF) as the EU standard for the development of information systems,[134] and the creation of 'automated data quality control mechanisms and procedures'.[135]

Although interoperability has been presented as a purely technical choice by the Commission, others have argued that it has the potential to constitute a *paradigm shift* for data collection, processing, and sharing across the EU information systems,[136] which is especially pertinent in the context of data used for law enforcement purposes. The EDPS has stressed that introducing interoperability is a profoundly political choice,[137] and it will result in a central database of third country nationals, complete with a central biometric register, making it all the more vulnerable and prone to be subject to abuse.[138] The apparent underlying aims of centralisation and unification seem to be already influencing the EU information systems landscape: as has been stated above,[139] the

128 EDPS para 11, Interoperability Regulation art 6.

129 Interoperability Regulation arts 4(10) and 12; EDPS para 12. This data will consist of biometric data included in the SIS or the Common Identity Repository.

130 Interoperability Regulation preamble para 26.

131 Interoperability Regulation art 17.

132 Interoperability Regulation arts 25 as well as 30–33.

133 Interoperability Regulation art 39.

134 Interoperability Regulation art 38.

135 Interoperability Regulation art 37.

136 According to the EDPS, para 25, it will mark 'a point of no return'.

137 EDPS para 25.

138 EDPS para 28 and 31; Reinhard Kreissl, 'Will More Data Bring More Security? Remarks on the Security Union Approach to Interoperability' in *Constitutionalising* 97–98.

139 See section 1.

development of EU information systems has been recently recalibrated in order to better fit the requirements and objectives of interoperability. For instance, ECRIS-TCN has been revised from its initial conception as a decentralised system modelled after ECRIS to a central system that will be interoperability-ready.[140] Despite the original intentions of its developers, interoperability will in fact result in pooling data (or templates of data), in establishing new access rights,[141] and in providing new centralised databases—even though these will initially not concern EU citizens, but rather third country nationals.

What is more, in the original Proposal for the Interoperability Regulation, it was explicitly noted that the new CIR aimed to streamline 'access of law enforcement officials to non-law enforcement information systems' when this was 'necessary for the prevention, investigation, detection and prosecution of serious crime'.[142] Under the Interoperability Regulation, this trend continues, as Europol and designated national authorities may also consult the CIR 'where necessary for the prevention, detection or investigation of terrorist offences or other serious criminal offences'.[143] As in the case of the underlying information systems, terrorism is defined as the acts described or acts equivalent to those described in the relevant Directive on combating terrorism [*Directive (EU) 2017/541*] and serious crime is defined as a wide spectrum of crimes indicated in the Framework Decision on the European Arrest Warrant [*2002/584/JHA*].[144] It is evident that this wording seems unacceptably vague,[145] especially by criminal law standards and in light of the fact that no concrete conditions are provided upon which law enforcement authorities may exercise their right of access. This is particularly troubling when it refers to sensitive data like biometric data. Among the most prominent changes in this respect is the fact that, according to the Interoperability Regulation, police authorities may be given the power to casually query the CIR with biometric data for the purposes of an identity check[146] and according to a two-step match-flag process meant to serve as a guarantee.[147]

It is also interesting to note that the systems that interoperability will encompass are in different stages of development so far. The Regulations on Interoperability cover *systems already functioning* (SIS, Eurodac and VIS),

140 See section 1.2.
141 EDPS para 145.
142 Interoperability Proposal art 17.
143 Interoperability Regulation arts 17 and 22.
144 Interoperability Regulation art 4(21),(22).
145 EDPS para 40.
146 Interoperability Regulation art 20.
147 Interoperability Regulation preamble paras 32–36.

along with systems newly established and *under construction* (EES, ETIAS and ECRIS-TCN). Therefore, some of the elements of the new regime are not sufficiently defined yet, while existing systems are not without fault and they are all currently under revision—which makes it impossible to know exactly how they will look when they become interoperable. In light of this, it is arguable that introducing interoperability may magnify existing problems or issues that might occur when the newer systems become operational. Furthermore, it must be stressed that while interoperability is intrinsically linked to the objective of contributing to *a high level of security* in the EU,[148] its implementation mostly incorporates systems that primarily focus on border control and immigration management.[149]

4 *National Transposition—the Example of the Greek Legal Order*

Finally, in order to better appreciate the effect of EU legislation regarding information sharing, the example of the main aspects of the Greek legislation applying or transposing the acts examined herein is briefly presented. In general, the impact on the Greek legislation *verifies* the effect of information sharing on criminal law, most notably due to enabling the processing of DNA samples as evidence in the context of criminal proceedings and using information on past convictions handed abroad when referring to criminal records.

More specifically, first of all, in Greece, duties concerning the operation of information systems are largely allocated to *the Police*.[150] With regard to *SIS* in particular, Greece has indeed reserved access rights for many national authorities, and more specifically the Police, border authorities, customs authorities, judicial authorities competent to prosecute criminal offences and to conduct judicial inquiries, authorities competent to grant visas and/or residence permits, and authorities competent to issue motor vehicles registration documents. On the other hand, information exchange within the context of *ECRIS* involves the Greek Ministry of Justice.[151] In the process of incorporating the ECRIS FD, Greece *amended* the national provision on the information included in the criminal record regarding the identity of a person and *expanded its scope*.[152] Moreover, it accompanies the transmission of convictions with almost the widest range of information possible as provided

148 Interoperability Regulation art 2(1)(c).

149 The Eurodac, the VIS, the EES, the ETIAS and the SIS (which pursues both objectives).

150 See mainly Presidential decree 178/2014 art 8.

151 Law 4360/2016 art 21.

152 Law 4360/2016 art 33 amended art 574 of the Greek Code of Criminal Procedure which was in force at the time; the content of the provision is repeated in the new art 569 of the current version of the Greek Code of Criminal Procedure.

for by the EU legislation (the most notable exception being not transmitting fingerprint data).[153]

Furthermore, based on Council Decision (EU) 2017/617, Greece is entitled to receive and supply personal data for the purposes of automated searching and comparison of DNA data, pursuant to articles 3 and 4 of the *Prüm* Decision, as from 2 April 2017; similarly, based on Council Decision (EU) 2017/1868, it is entitled to receive and supply dactyloscopic data, pursuant to article 9 of the Prüm Decision, as from as from 18 October 2017. Originally, the Greek legislation did not cover the collection of DNA samples in the context of criminal proceedings. The need to comply with the Prüm Decision led to the respective *amendment* of the Greek Code of Criminal Procedure in 2009[154] and to the addition of a provision[155] of extremely controversial character.[156] Finally, the transposition of the *PNR Directive* was recently concluded with the adoption of Law 4579/2018 (Greece had already incorporated the API Directive in 2008).[157] The Greek legislator acknowledges the importance of collecting and exchanging PNR data, mostly in view of the fact that the law applies to both extra-EU *and to intra-EU flights*,[158] and that the authorities to be granted the right to request such data for the purpose of processing it and subsequently detecting, preventing and investigating serious criminal offences are defined very widely, involving judicial authorities, the Police, customs authorities, the Fire Department, the Agency responsible for internal security and other special task forces.[159]

---

153 Law 4360/2016 art 23.

154 Law 3783/2009 art 12(3).

155 Art 200A, whose provisions are repeated in art 201 of the Greek Code of Criminal Procedure currently in force. The competent authority to store DNA samples is the Hellenic Police Forensic Science Division (Presidential decree 178/2014 art 30).

156 Among the various problematic aspects of the issue (see also section 8), intense controversy was fuelled in Greece by the (potentially) coercive character of the measure, which is extremely intrusive to the human body; criticism includes arguments referring to the coercive collection of DNA samples as *torture and direct disregard of human dignity and of the value of a human being*, which is protected under art 2 of the Greek Constitution, and in any case of the presumption of innocence; see indicatively [in Greek] Lampros Margaritis, 'Analysis and Coersion', and Elisavet Symeonidou-Kastanidou, 'DNA Analysis and criminal trial: the European institutional framework', both in *DNA analysis* 199ff and 12ff respectively; Ioannis Manoledakis, *Security and Freedom* (Sakkoulas 2002) 157–158; Stergios Alexiadis, *Crime Investigation* (Sakkoulas 2006) 264; Panagiotis Kaisaris in Lampros Margaritis, *Code of Criminal Procedure* (Nomiki Bibiliothiki 2011) 736; Argyrios Karras, *Code of Criminal Procedure* (3rd edn, Nomiki Bibiliothiki 2016) 353–354.

157 By virtue of Presidential Decree 53/2008.

158 Law 4579/2018 arts 1 and 2.

159 Law 4579/2018 art 9.

5 *Main Points of Concern*

Evidently, information collecting, processing and sharing is currently an evolving field of EU law that is connected to criminal law in a *firm and multileveled* manner. To this extent, having presented and concisely commented on the identifying elements of the information systems operating in the EU area of police and judicial cooperation in criminal matters and their national aspects in the example of Greece, as well as the most significant related development (i.e. interoperability), this paper aims to assess the most important problems and challenges that arise in the above field. The ultimate goal of this evaluation is to thoroughly address issues that may at first appear to only involve immigration control or even police cooperation, but are revealed to be *particularly linked to criminal law*, which, albeit one of the most significant aspects of the subject, is often underestimated.

In this context, *guarantees* related to preventing abuse and disproportionate storage and processing of data, along with the rules on *personal data protection* are of unique importance. An apparent reason concerns the fact that, due to the terrorist hits in various EU countries, many citizens are willing to accept serious restrictions to their right to privacy for the sake of security, and even more people are willing to accept *exceptional measures of controversial nature* to apply to specific groups of people (e.g. third country nationals, ex-convicts, etc.). Besides these dilemmas regarding the protection of personal rights, one must consider another aspect of the link between data collecting and criminal law, and examine whether processing personal data affects the essential characteristics of modern criminal law and perhaps even its fundamental features and principles.

Part 2. Evaluation of the EU Framework on the Collection, Processing and Exchange of Personal Data for Criminal Law Purposes: Principles, Limitations and Safeguards

6 *Defining the Criminal Law Purposes Served by the Collection, Processing and Exchange of Personal Data*

In the effort to evaluate in depth the relationship between criminal law and the information storage and sharing conducted through the systems operating within the framework of judicial cooperation in criminal matters and police cooperation in the EU, it is essential to keep in mind the specific *objectives* pursued in the context of each information system and in relation to criminal law. Obviously, even the same data, e.g. on past convictions, plays a different role when exchanged for the purpose of applying the rules on recidivism and defining the appropriate penalty to impose on a person charged with committing a criminal offence,[160] than when it is the basis to consider a person as a potential future offender.[161] Thus, it is of unique importance to primarily confirm the extent to which *data is used to punish offences or to prevent individuals from committing ones*. In this respect, it is crucial to especially explore the connection between data processing and *preventive criminal law*;[162] since the EU legislator has gone as far as requiring the criminalisation of 'neutral' acts, justifying this choice solely in view of the intention of the individuals that perform these acts to commit other criminal offences in the future, any data used within criminal proceedings to reveal such intentions may in the end function as the *decisive evidence* against the person accused.

Taking into consideration the above, one may categorise *the purposes* served by the use of data (as described in Part 1) *depending on their connection to criminal proceedings* and the stage of the latter; under this criterion, the following categories could be formed:

a. Data to be used *after the conclusion* of criminal proceedings and in relation to a *judgment or a sentence* for a criminal offence;[163]
b. Data to be used *during the sentencing stage within* criminal proceedings;[164]

---

160 See preamble para 2 and art 3(2) of Framework Decision 2008/675/JHA.

161 See Europol Regulation Annex II.B.(2)(j)(i), according to which information on previous convictions may be collected for the purpose of operational analyses (= with the aim of supporting criminal investigations) for persons regarding whom there are factual indications or reasonable grounds under the national law to believe that they will commit criminal offences; see also ECRIS-TCN Regulation preamble para 2.

162 See the development of different aspects of 'preventive criminal law' in Ulrich Sieber, 'The new architecture in Security Law: Crime control in the global risk society' in Ulrich Sieber and others (eds), *Alternative Systems of Crime Control: National, Transnational, and International Dimensions* (Duncker & Humblot 2018) (*Alternative Systems*) 5ff; Kaiafa-Gbandi, 'Information exchange' 146.

163 Such data can be found in European arrest warrants or arrest warrants based on international agreements, which are issued in order for the convicted person to be surrendered or extradited *so as to serve a penalty*; it also involves data for the purpose of communicating the place of residence of persons who are *to be served a criminal judgment or to be summoned in order to serve a penalty* (SIS II Decision arts 26 and 34 respectively), as well as past convictions, which may affect the rules governing *the execution of a decision* [art 3(2) Framework Decision 2008/675/JHA], or *the application of the exclusions emanating from Directive 2011/93/EU* [ECRIS FD art 7, ECRIS Directive preamble para 10, ECRIS-TCN Regulation art 7(1) and Directive 2011/93/EU art 10], when a conviction specifically concerns sexual offences against minors.

164 This category involves data on past convictions to be used *to define the appropriate penalty* to impose on a person that is convicted of committing a criminal offence (ECRIS FD art 7).

c. Data to be used *in the context or in view* of criminal proceedings;[165]
d. Data to be used for the '*investigation*' of criminal offences;[166]
e. Data to be used for the '*prevention*' of criminal offences.[167]

Therefore, since it is clearly established that data stored in the EU information systems is indeed used in relation to criminal cases, it is subsequently critical to determine whether the collection and the processing of the data *adheres to the fundamental guarantees* that must be respected with regard to such use.

---

165 This includes data found in European arrest warrants or arrest warrants based on international agreements, which are issued in order for a person to be surrendered or extradited *so as to stand trial*; also, data for the purpose of communicating the place of residence of *witnesses*, or of persons to appear before judicial authorities *when prosecuted* or to be served documents related to their prosecution; moreover, it covers data on objects connected to criminal proceedings, *to be seized or used as evidence* (SIS II Decision arts 26, 34 and 38 respectively); finally, it covers data on past convictions, which may affect *the applicable rules of procedure at the pre-trial stage*, such as the rules on provisional detention, or be important as to *the definition of the criminal offence*, eg in the case of recurrent offences [Framework Decision 2008/675/JHA art 3(2)].

166 This category includes: the entire set of data collected by Europol for the purpose of *operational* analysis (= for supporting criminal investigations) and for *cross-checking* [Europol Regulation arts 2(c) and 18, Annex II.A and B respectively]; data for the purpose of *discreet or specific checks* on persons in view of prosecuting criminal offences, where there is 'clear indication' that *they are committing* a serious criminal offence, and data on objects connected to serious criminal offences [SIS II Decision arts 36 and 38 respectively]; data on past convictions (ECRIS FD art 7); PNR data (PNR Directive Annex I); DNA data, dactyloscopic data, vehicle registration data (Prüm Decision arts 2, 8, 12), as well as fingerprints, photographs and alphanumerical identity data from the immigration databases [VIS Regulation art 5; Eurodac Regulation arts 11, 14; EES Regulation arts 15–18; ETIAS Regulation art 17].

167 This category covers: the types of data collected by Europol for the purpose of *strategic* analysis and for *cross-checking* [Europol Regulation arts 2(c) and 18, Annex II.A and B respectively]; data for the purpose of *discreet or specific checks*, where there is 'clear indication' that a person *intends to commit* a serious criminal offence, or where an 'overall assessment' of a person gives reason to suppose that *he/she will commit* serious criminal offences in the future, and data on objects connected to serious criminal offences [SIS II Decision arts 36 and 38 respectively]; personal data, where final convictions or other circumstances give reason to believe that the subject *will commit criminal offences during major events with a cross-border dimension* (namely European Council meetings or sporting events) (Prüm Decision art 14), or *a terrorist offence* (Prüm Decision arts 8, 12, 16); past convictions concerning sexual offences against minors so as to *prevent offenders from working* with children [ECRIS FD art 7, ECRIS Directive preamble para 10, ECRIS-TCN Regulation art 7(1) and Directive 2011/93/EU art 10]; PNR data (PNR Directive Annex I); dactyloscopic data, vehicle registration data and identity data (Prüm Decision arts 8, 12, 16), and fingerprints, photographs and alphanumerical identity data from the immigration databases [VIS Regulation art 5; Eurodac Regulation arts 11 and 14; EES Regulation arts 15–18; ETIAS Regulation art 17].

This task, of course, first of all entails examining *the guarantees deriving from personal data protection rules*. However, it further requires assessing *the fundamental principles and rights that govern criminal procedure*. In this context, it is obvious that, when data results from a criminal procedure (e.g. from a conviction or from issuing an arrest warrant) and is to be used in the context of one (a trial or a pre-trial investigation), these procedural guarantees normally apply. On the contrary, when the source of the data is irrelevant to a criminal procedure (e.g. PNR data or identification data from immigration control databases) or is at some point decisively processed outside the context of a criminal procedure (e.g. a conviction that Europol assesses to clearly indicate that the person in question may commit an offence in the future), the discussion as to whether criminal procedure guarantees apply is open;[168] and the stronger the role of the data in the criminal proceedings that may follow (as in the case where preventive objectives are pursued through criminalisation), the more intense the discussion.

Still, it is necessary to go even further. The present study has been faced with the troubling finding that data collection and processing which supplement criminal law objectives may fall within an area *preceding* the latter's clear scope (as will be explained in depth under section 9); that is, in an area where criminal law fundamental principles and rights do not prima facie appear to apply. Given the *recent developments and the future perspectives concerning this activity*, which include enhancing and expanding information exchange at the EU level,[169] as well as gradually adopting (mainly at national level) controversial *police law* measures that directly follow the assessment of information and serve preventive purposes,[170] this study seeks, as a final point, to determine

168 See for example related points regarding *intelligence materials* that are used as evidence and the issue of revealing them to the defendant (= person under surveillance) in the context of fulfilling the 'equality of arms' principle in Lorena Bachmaier, 'Countering terrorism: Suspects without suspicion and (pre-)suspects under surveillance' in *Alternative Systems* 187f.

169 See above the Introduction and sections 1 and 3.

170 See Sieber in *Alternative Systems* 12, who discusses police law measures that pursue preventive objectives 'with sanction-like legal consequences', which have increased in Germany; the author refers to new 'control sanctions' (restraining orders, orders not to go to/leave a certain location, obligations to personally and regularly appear at a police station etc) and 'control networks' for repeat offenders, and most notably to the amendments occurred with regard to preventive custody in Bavaria, which since 2018 can last up to three months based on a judicial decision 'if a certain level of danger has been reached' and can be extended for up to three months at a time (on this also <https://edri.org/bavarians-protest-against-vastly-extended-police-powers/> accessed 1 February 2020).

safeguards and limitations that can indeed function at a stage which the rules on criminal procedure do not traditionally cover.

To this end, analysis in this section involves *EU* law with regard to personal data protection, criminal law and police cooperation; references to *Greek* criminal law and to Greek 'police law', meant to serve as an example of national legislation; and certain references to other legal orders where appropriate, notably *US* law, in order to provide insight from a legal order which has a distinctive stance in the areas of personal data protection and combating terrorism, and which collaborates with the EU in key issues that include information sharing.[171]

7 *Principles, Rights and Limitations that Stem from Data Protection Legislation*

7.1 Data Protection Principles: the Legal Framework in the Case of EU Information Systems

As has been outlined above, the data collected and processed by the information systems examined in the scope of this paper can be used for law enforcement and judicial purposes at various stages of the criminal justice systems. Furthermore, databases like the Prüm Framework or the Europol systems were established with express criminal law purposes, while even information systems with the primary purpose of regulating migration, like VIS, EES and ETIAS, include provisions on using the data stored for the purposes of preventing and combating crime, most notably terrorism and what is described as 'serious crime'.[172]

While collecting, processing and sharing information is considered of paramount importance for promoting security within the EU area, there are certain limits that delineate the boundaries within which this activity can be carried out. The first set of limits can be found in the principles of data protection, which safeguard the privacy and autonomy of the persons whose personal data is collected (data subjects).

It is important to note that exceptions are often made in the context of fundamental data protection principles when the information is collected or used for preventing, investigating and combating crime. In this context, the data protection principles will only be examined within the scope of criminal law purposes and in the context of the information systems examined in this

---

171 See for example Agreement between the USA and the EU on the use and transfer of passenger name records to the US Department of Homeland Security [2012] OJ L 215/5.

172 A very broad spectrum of crimes are considered 'serious crimes'. For more on this, see the critical remarks under sections 2.2 and 3 above.

paper. After all, invoking criminal law purposes can have a twofold impact on data protection principles. On the one part, it can lead to permissible derogations from data protection principles, since criminal law authorities must by definition be awarded certain extended and intrusive powers, compared to other public authorities, in order to carry out their function of preventing and combating crime. On the other part, it can be used to argue in favour of an added layer of limitations in order to reinforce data protection principles, since the consequences of abuse of power by criminal justice authorities can have a far-reaching and onerous impact on the individual.

The data protection principles that are relevant in the context of the information systems in this paper can be found in two broader sets of rules. On a first level, these principles are enshrined in special legal rules contained within the legal frameworks examined herein, i.e. the legal acts establishing and regulating the information systems. These provisions act as *lex specialis* with regard to the rights and obligations enshrined under them.

On a second level, when a matter is not regulated under the provisions contained in those legal acts, we should turn to relevant EU data protection legislation that constitutes *lex generalis* with regard to the information systems and the data subject rights. In this case, the most relevant EU legal instruments are Directive (EU) 2016/680 on the protection of natural persons with regard to the processing of personal data by competent authorities for the purposes of the prevention, investigation, detection or prosecution of criminal offences or the execution of criminal penalties, and on the free movement of such data,[173] which will be examined in more detail below, the General Data Protection Regulation (GDPR),[174] and Regulation (EU) 2018/1725.[175] Between the first two,

173 Directive (EU) 2016/680 of 27 April 2016 [2016] OJ L 119/89. In May 2018, this Directive repealed Framework Decision 2008/977/JHA of 27 November 2008 on the protection of personal data processed in the framework of police and judicial cooperation in criminal matters [2008] OJ L 350/60, which had regulated the matter until then.

174 Regulation (EU) 2016/679 of 27 April 2016 on the protection of natural persons with regard to the processing of personal data and on the free movement of such data, and repealing Directive 95/46/ EC (*General Data Protection Regulation*), [2016] OJ L 119/1 [GDPR].

175 Regulation (EU) 2018/1725 of 23 October 2018 on the protection of natural persons with regard to the processing of personal data by the Union institutions, bodies, offices and agencies and on the free movement of such data, and repealing Regulation (EC) No 45/2001 and Decision No 1247/2002/ EC [2001] OJ L 295/39, which replaced Regulation (EC) 45/2001 in December 2018. Art 2(3) of Directive (EU) 2016/680 explains that the Directive 'does not apply to the processing of personal data: (a) in the course of an activity which falls outside the scope of Union law; (b) by the Union institutions, bodies, offices and agencies'. Art 2(3) of the GDPR also states 'processing of personal data by the Union institutions,

Directive (EU) 2016/680 is *lex specialis* with regard to the GDPR in the context of processing data for the purposes of preventing and combating crime, since the GDPR explicitly states under article 2(2)(d) that its material scope does not include 'processing of personal data by competent authorities for the purposes of the prevention, investigation, detection or prosecution of criminal offences or the execution of criminal penalties, including the safeguarding against and the prevention of threats to public security'. Any matters that are still left unregulated after applying the specialised provisions in the legal acts setting up the information systems and then the Directive (EU) 2016/680 will fall under the ambit of the GDPR and its provisions, which are broader in scope.

Last but not least, it is important to recognise the role of Regulation (EU) 2018/1725 as another piece of the puzzle in the case of data protection rules that apply as *lex generalis* in the case of EU information systems. Regulation (EU) 2018/1725 replaced the long-standing Regulation (EC) 45/2001 in regulating the processing of personal data by the institutions, bodies, offices and agencies of the EU itself. What is most relevant in the context of this paper is that, contrary to the previous regime, Regulation (EU) 2018/1725 will apply to Eurojust as soon as the agency reform is completed and starting in 2022; its provisions will also apply to Europol and the European Public Prosecutor's Office.[176]

The distinction between *lex specialis* and *lex generalis* in the context of EU data protection law and specifically in the case of personal data protection safeguards with regard to EU information systems, as well as its underlying principle of *lex specialis derogat legi generali*, are well-established in EU legal instruments[177] and in the opinions of the EDPS.[178] In particular, in the context

bodies, offices and agencies' falls outside the scope of the GDPR. For an explanation of why the EU has chosen to keep this 'fragmented structure' instead of taking the opportunity in the context of the recent reforms to set up a 'unified' legal framework, as well as an account of the function and the importance of data protection authorities monitoring police and criminal justice authorities, see Paul de Hert and Juraj Sajfert 'The role of Data Protection Authorities in supervising police and criminal justice authorities processing personal data' in Chloe Briere and Anne Weyembergh (eds), *The Needed Balances in EU Criminal Law: Past, Present and Future* (Hart Publishing 2018) 244–247.

176 European Parliament 'Press Release 13–09–2018' <www.europarl.europa.eu/news/en/press-room/20180906IPR12126/stronger-data-protection-rules-for-eu-institutions-and-agencies> accessed 2 February 2020.

177 See eg Regulation (EU) 2018/1725 preamble para 11.

178 EDPS, 'Opinion of the European Data Protection Supervisor on the Proposal for a Framework Decision on the protection of personal data processed in the framework of police and judicial co-operation in criminal matters' [2006] OJ C 47/27 para II.3.20.

of pinpointing the different layers of personal data protection with regard to SIS II, the EDPS noted that the pertinent legal framework was 'very complex' and 'based on the combined application of *lex generalis* and *lex specialis*', while in the same opinion he also warned that 'the combined application of different legal instruments should lead neither to discrepancies between national regimes on fundamental aspects, nor to a watering down of the present level of data protection'.[179] In doing so, the EDPS identified a considerable risk that the creation of such a complex landscape with many different layers and applicable instruments with regard to data protection might lead to reduced efficiency in terms of protecting the individuals concerned. This trend of creating a complicated data protection regime is unfortunately replicated in the other EU information systems examined under this paper, which means that there is little hope for this risk to be effectively mitigated. It is crucial at this point to turn our attention on each of these data protection levels to evaluate their scope and the safeguards they provide.

7.2 *Lex Specialis*: Safeguards Contained in the Legal Acts Setting Up and Regulating the Information Systems

The scope of lawful processing of personal data for criminal law purposes is limited by the rights of the data subject, which are laid out in specific provisions in the legislative documents setting up the information systems examined in this paper. A comparative overview of these provisions reveals that, in the context of the data processed by the information systems examined here for criminal law purposes,[180] data subjects enjoy the right of access,[181]

179 EDPS, 'Opinion of the European Data Protection Supervisor on the Proposal for a Council Decision on the establishment, operation and use of the Second Generation Schengen Information System (SIS II)' [2006] OJ C 91/38 para 1.2. Also, Franziska Boehm, *Information Sharing and Data Protection in the Area of Freedom, Security and Justice* (Spinger 2012) 273–274.

180 No such specific provisions are included in Council Decision 2009/316/JHA nor in the ECRIS FD.

181 Directive (EU) 2016/680 art 14; Prüm Decision art 31; PNR Directive art 13(1); Europol Regulation art 36; SIS II Decision art 58(1); Regulation (EC) No 1987/2006 art 41; Eurodac Regulation art 29; VIS Decision art 14(1); VIS Regulation art 38(1); EES Regulation art 52; ETIAS Regulation art 64; SIS Regulation art 67; Regulation (EU) 2018/1861 art 53; ECRIS-TCN Regulation art 25.

right of rectification,[182] right of erasure,[183] and right of restriction,[184] as well as the right to lodge a complaint and seek judicial remedies including compensation for damages.[185] It is important to note in respect with the rights to lodge a complaint, as well as seek remedy and compensation for unlawful processing, that it is often unclear to the data subjects how and at which forum these rights can be exercised. The existence of different levels and institutional frameworks for the exercise of these rights, which can vary wildly, ranging from EU organs to national authorities, as well as the occasional existence of other obstacles, such as the fact that certain EU organs like Europol may enjoy certain privileges and immunities which have to be tackled before data subjects can take up their claims, makes the landscape especially confusing and uncertain for those wishing to exercise such rights, effectively hindering their application.[186]

Provisions under the information systems legislative documents also provide for certain retention periods for the personal data collected. In some cases, a very short retention period is provided for before the data is deleted, such as 24 hours for API data,[187] unless the data is needed for longer, or depersonalised, such as six months in the case of the PNR Directive.[188] In other

182 Directive (EU) 2016/680 art 16(1); Prüm Decision art 31; PNR Directive art 13(1); Europol Regulation art 37(1); SIS II Decision art 58(5); Regulation (EC) No 1987/2006 art 41; Eurodac Regulation art 29(5); VIS Decision art 14(5); VIS Regulation art 38(2); EES Regulation art 52; ETIAS Regulation art 64; SIS Regulation art 67; Regulation (EU) 2018/1861 art 53; Regulation (EU) 2018/1861 art 53; ECRIS-TCN Regulation art 25.

183 Directive (EU) 2016/680 art 16(2); Prüm Decision art 31; PNR Directive art 13(1); Europol Regulation art 37(2); SIS II Decision art 58(5); Regulation (EC) No 1987/2006 art 41; Eurodac Regulation art 29(5); VIS Decision art 14(5); VIS Regulation art 38(2); EES Regulation art 52 EU; ETIAS Regulation art 64; SIS Regulation art 67; Regulation (EU) 2018/1861 art 53; ECRIS-TCN Regulation art 25.

184 Directive (EU) 2016/680 art 16(3); PNR Directive art 13(1); Europol Regulation art 37(3); EES Regulation art 52; ETIAS Regulation art 64; SIS Regulation art 67; Regulation (EU) 2018/1861 art 53; ECRIS-TCN Regulation art 25.

185 Directive (EU) 2016/680 art 16(4); Prüm Decision art 31; PNR Directive art 13(1); Europol Regulation arts 47, 49 and 50; SIS II Decision art 59; Regulation (EC) No 1987/2006 art 43; Eurodac Regulation art 29(8),(15); VIS Decision arts 11 and 14(8); VIS Regulation art 40, EES Regulation art 54 EU; ETIAS Regulation art 64; SIS Regulation art 68; Regulation (EU) 2018/1861 art 54; ECRIS-TCN Regulation art 27.

186 See also on this issue Kaiafa-Gbandi, 'Coordinating organs' 165–177.

187 API Directive art 6(1).

188 Art 12.

cases, such as in the Europol Regulation,[189] the SIS II Decision,[190] and the SIS Regulation,[191] data can be stored for 'as long as necessary and proportionate for the purposes for which it was collected', with regular review periods. Under the Eurodac Regulation, retention periods may vary from 18 months[192] to ten years,[193] while the retention period for VIS, EES and ETIAS is typically up to a maximum of five years.[194] Finally, the Prüm Decision refers to 'the maximum period for keeping data laid down in the national law of the supplying Member State',[195] while under the ECRIS-TCN Regulation data records are kept in the central system 'for as long as the data related to the convictions of the person concerned are stored in the criminal records'.[196]

Data subject rights and retention period provisions are pivotal in safeguarding that the use of personal data by law enforcement and judicial authorities will not be abused. Yet, in order for data subject rights to act as effective safeguards, it is important for data subjects to both know that they have these rights and what they consist of, as well as how to exercise them efficiently and without added obstacles, as has been noted above. Furthermore, since adhering to data protection principles and data retention periods is a process that is in large part carried out internally by the authorities that process the data, checks and balances must be put in place in each case in order to ensure that the relevant provisions are properly enforced. Only if exercised and applied efficiently can data protection principles, data subject rights and data retention provisions add another layer of limitations to law enforcement and criminal justice activity.

7.3 *Lex Generalis*: Safeguards Contained in Broader EU Legislation

As mentioned, at the EU level, Directive (EU) 2016/680 regulates processing personal data in the context of law enforcement. First of all, it must be clarified that personal data means any information that relates to an identified or identifiable natural person.[197] Furthermore, in addition to the specialised

189 Art 37(1),(2).

190 SIS II Decision art 44 for alerts on persons and art 45 for alerts on objects; also Regulation (EC) No 1987/2006 art 29.

191 SIS Regulation arts 53 and 54, which state that alerts on persons and on objects respectively 'shall be kept only for the time required to achieve the purposes for which they were entered'. See also Regulation (EU) 2018/1861 art 39 with the same wording.

192 Eurodac Regulation art 16.

193 Eurodac Regulation art 12.

194 VIS Regulation art 23; EES Regulation art 34; ETIAS Regulation art 54.

195 Prüm Decision art 27(3).

196 ECRIS-TCN Regulation art 8.

197 Directive (EU) 2016/680 art 3.

provisions cited above for each information system, data subject rights are also laid down in articles 12–18 of Directive (EU) 2016/680.[198]

Secondly, it must be noted that Directive (EU) 2016/680 has limitations in its scope of application, as it does not apply to EU legal acts in the field of judicial cooperation in criminal matters and police cooperation that were already in force on or before 6 May 2016, as article 60 of the Directive explicitly states.[199] This means that, for instance, the Prüm Treaty provisions that were transposed under Council Decision 2008/615/JHA and refer to national law with regard to processing personal data remain in force.[200] In addition, article 2(3) of Directive (EU) 2016/680 also explicitly states, as already mentioned, that its scope does not include processing by EU institutions, bodies, offices and agencies,[201] or processing in the course of an activity which falls outside the scope of EU law.

Even with these limitations in mind, Directive (EU) 2016/680 sets the tone for the rules governing data processing for criminal law purposes, while its principles also in large part correspond to the general data protection principles laid down in the GDPR. More specifically, according to article 4 of the Directive, which lays out the 'principles relating to processing of personal data', this data must be:

(a) processed lawfully and fairly (*principle of lawfulness and fairness*),
(b) collected for specified, explicit and legitimate purposes and not processed in a manner that is incompatible with those purposes (*principle of purpose limitation*),
(c) adequate, relevant and not excessive in relation to the purposes for which it is processed (*principle of data minimisation*),
(d) accurate and, where necessary, kept up to date, while every reasonable step must be taken to ensure that personal data that is inaccurate, having regard to the purposes for which it is processed, is erased or rectified without delay (*principle of accuracy*),

198 See also GDPR arts 12–23 and arts 17–24 of Regulation (EU) 2018/1725, which include further data subject rights, such as the right to data portability.

199 Directive (EU) 2016/680 art 60 ('Union legal acts already in force') provides for the following: 'The specific provisions for the protection of personal data in Union legal acts that entered into force on or before 6 May 2016 in the field of judicial cooperation in criminal matters and police cooperation, which regulate processing between Member States and the access of designated authorities of Member States to information systems established pursuant to the Treaties within the scope of this Directive, shall remain unaffected'.

200 See on this note Kaiafa-Gbandi, 'Information exchange' 152–153.

201 These are as a rule governed by Regulation (EU) 2018/1725.

(e) kept in a form which permits identification of data subjects for no longer than is necessary for the purposes for which it is processed (*principle of storage limitation*),

(f) processed in a manner that ensures appropriate security of the personal data, including protection against unauthorised or unlawful processing and against accidental loss, destruction or damage, using appropriate technical or organisational measures (*principles of integrity and confidentiality*).

These principles correspond to the content of the relevant principles laid out in article 5 of the GDPR,[202] the flagship EU legislation on personal data protection that regulates the protection of natural persons with regard to the processing of personal data and the free movement of data.[203] One notable exception is the principle of transparency enshrined in the GDPR,[204] which further provides that personal data must be 'processed (...) in a transparent manner in relation to the data subject'. The absence of this principle is not surprising when it comes to law enforcement and judicial authorities, which must at the investigative stage mainly act in secrecy, especially with regard to a data subject who is a suspect or accused of a crime. With regard to the principle of lawfulness and fairness,[205] it establishes the basis for law enforcement action, which must be exercised according to the relevant legislation and not in a manner which constitutes abuse of power. The principles of purpose limitation, data minimisation and storage limitation refer to key aspects of the same underlying principle: that law enforcement authorities may not gather, process and store more data than they should and need to. This includes stating the binding purposes for which they will collect and process data in advance

202 For more on the GDPR, see, inter alia, Andreas Linder (ed), *European Data Protection Law: General Data Protection Regulation 2016* (CreateSpace 2016); Paul Voigt and Axel von dem Bussche, *The EU General Data Protection Regulation (GDPR)—A Practical Guide* (Springer 2017); Feiler L, Forgó N and Weigl M, *The EU General Data Protection Regulation (GDPR): A Commentary* (Globe Law & Business 2018); Denis Kelleher and Karen Murray, *EU Data Protection Law* (Bloomsbury 2018); Lilian Mitrou, *The General Data Protection Regulation* [in Greek] (Sakkoulas 2017); Ioannis Igglezakis, *The General Data Protection Regulation (Regulation 2016/679)* [in Greek] (Interactive Books 2018).

203 See GDPR arts 1 and 2 for its scope and exceptions thereto.

204 It is also important to note that there are other dissimilarities between the two instruments, based on their scope; for instance, consent is understandably not used as widely by Directive (EU) 2016/680 as a legal basis for data processing as in the context of the GDPR. See on this Magdalena Kedzior, 'GDPR and beyond—a year of changes in the data protection landscape of the European Union' [2019] ERA Forum 505, 508.

205 Damian Clifford and Jef Ausloos, 'Data Protection and the Role of Fairness' (CiTiP Working Paper 29/2017, August 3 2017 <https://ssrn.com/abstract=3013139> accessed 2 February 2020).

(purpose limitation), processing only the data that is necessary for these purposes (data minimisation), and keeping them for no longer than is required for these purposes (storage limitation).

Finally, law enforcement authorities must make sure that the data processed is accurate (principle of accuracy), as well as secure and protected against unauthorised access (principles of integrity and confidentiality). These fundamental data protection principles are vested with added importance in the field of criminal law. For instance, it is particularly crucial that law enforcement and judicial authorities keep accurate data in order to ensure that suspects or accused, who will be subjected to the vigorous process of being investigated with regard to a crime, are correctly identified. Furthermore, when it comes to sensitive data like criminal convictions, it is even more important to adhere to the principle of security and confidentiality and make sure that all steps are taken to prevent unauthorised access.

Within the scope of this paper, the principle of purpose limitation has a particularly crucial role to play. As has been already explained above, information systems that were initially or primarily set up to serve specific purposes were extended to cover law enforcement purposes as well. This has in effect led to the following development, which raises concerns: information systems established with a specific purpose in mind, which did not relate to criminal law, were designed in a way that served this particular purpose, e.g. by collecting and processing a large volume and different types of data. When extending their purpose to cover criminal law objectives, without adding any further requirements, this essentially results in law enforcement authorities having access to a wider pool of data, since it is conceivable that if these systems have been set up from the start with criminal law purposes in mind, then they most probably would have been narrower in scope and would have included added safeguards. Thus, this unqualified mixing of purposes ends up in effectively circumventing the principle of purpose limitation.

Furthermore, the argument that the effectiveness of EU information systems is undermined by their 'fragmentation' has been put forward in order to justify the introduction of interoperability between the systems, as has been outlined above.[206] Yet this fragmentation is in part the result of applying the principle of purpose limitation, and while effectiveness is important, it should not be pursued at the expense of fundamental data protection principles.

Last but not least, there is some leeway for broader privacy legislation, like the GDPR or articles 7 and 8 of the Charter of Fundamental Rights of the European Union (Charter), which safeguard the right to private life and

206 See section 3.

the right to data protection respectively, to play a role in data processed for security purposes.

First of all, the GDPR regulates data protection by private bodies regarding information which could at a later stage be found to be of importance for law enforcement purposes. This is especially pertinent in the case of legislation implementing what has been dubbed as 'responsibilisation strategy',[207] i.e. the privatisation of certain tasks in combating crime and their delegating to nonstate actors like banks, lawyers, airlines etc., as is the case of PNR data.[208] Secondly, as the preamble of the GDPR points out,[209] 'competent authorities within the meaning of Directive (EU) 2016/680', which includes law enforcement agencies, may be entrusted by Member States with data processing in the context of tasks 'which are not necessarily carried out for the purposes of the prevention, investigation, detection or prosecution of criminal offences or the execution of criminal penalties, including the safeguarding against and prevention of threats to public security'. In those cases, that data processing activity will fall under the scope of the GDPR instead of Directive (EU) 2016/680. While this provision is aimed at regulating data processing e.g. for organisational reasons, it is conceivable that in some cases data not initially collected for crime prevention may at a later stage be found to be of interest for the prevention or investigation of a crime.

Finally, it must be noted that the Charter also protects the right to privacy and to data protection under articles 7 and 8 respectively. Article 8 in particular further expressly includes specific safeguards, such as the principles of fairness, legality, and purpose limitation, as well as the data subject rights to access and to rectification. After the Treaty of Lisbon was adopted in 2009, the Charter became a binding source of primary EU law, of the same legal value as the Treaties, as per article 6(1) TEU. The CJEU has further clarified the content of these rights through its case-law,[210] both before the Charter became binding[211] and afterwards,[212] recognising the right to data protection as a

207 David Garland, 'The Limits of the Sovereign State: Strategies of Crime Control in Contemporary Society' [1996] British Journal of Criminology 445–471; on this note, see also Mitsilegas in *Constitutionalising* 13.

208 Another notable example is money laundering legislation.

209 Para 19.

210 For an overview, see Maria Tzanou, *The Fundamental Right to Data Protection: Normative Value in the Context of Counter-Terrorism Surveillance* (Hart Publishing 2017) 48–62.

211 See eg Joined Cases C-465/00, C-138/01 and C-139/01 *Österreichischer Rundfunk and Others* EU:C:2003:294 ; Case C-101/01 *Lindqvist* EU:C:2003:596.

212 See eg Joined Cases *Volker und Markus Schecke GbR* (C-92/09) and *Hartmut Eifert* (C-93/09) v Land Hessen EU:C:2010:662; Case C-131/12 *Google Spain SL and Google Inc. v Agencia*

fundamental human right enshrined in the Charter for the first time in its *Promusicae* case in 2006.[213] The CJEU has routinely viewed the right to privacy and the right to data protection as connected,[214] but it has also had the chance to further refine the content of the right to data protection in the context of data gathered for the purposes of combating crime in seminal judgments such as *Digital Rights Ireland*,[215] *Schrems*,[216] and *Tele2 Sverige*.[217]

In *Digital Rights Ireland* in particular, CJEU turned its focus on communication data such as location and traffic data retained by service providers and highlighted that when this data is reviewed as a whole, it 'may allow very precise conclusions to be drawn concerning the private lives of the persons whose data has been retained' which includes 'the habits of everyday life, permanent or temporary places of residence, daily or other movements, the activities carried out, the social relationships of those persons and the social environments frequented by them',[218] thus emphasising the inherent risk posed by law enforcement surveillance activity. The CJEU confirmed these findings later in the *Tele2 Sverige* case, where it held again that traffic data allowed 'very precise conclusions to be drawn' about an individual's private life and was thus 'no less sensitive, having regard to the right to privacy, than the actual content of communications',[219] rendering the interference posed by such legislation 'particularly serious'.[220] The Court also drew a distinction between 'general and indiscriminate' retention of data for the purposes of combating crime, which it found unjustified,[221] and 'targeted' retention for the same

---

Española de Protección de Datos (AEPD) and Mario Costeja González EU:C:2014:317. In *Google Spain* in particular, the CJEU affirmed the 'right to be forgotten' in paras 96–99.

213 Case C-275/06 *Promusicae* EU:C:2008:54, para 63.

214 *Schecke*, para 47; Joined Cases C-468/10 and C-469/10 *ASNEF* EU:C:2011:777, para 42.

215 Joined Cases C-293/12 and C-594/12 *Digital Rights Ireland Ltd v Minister for Communications, Marine and Natural Resources and Others and Kärntner Landesregierung and Others* EU:C:2014:238.

216 Case C-362/14, *Maximillian Schrems v Data Protection Commissioner* (2014) ECLI:EU:C:2015:650. It must be noted that Case C-311/18 which is currently pending before the CJEU is a follow-up to the *Schrems* case, often referred to as *Schrems II*. In addition, Case T-738/16 *Quadrature du Net v. Commission*, which also challenges the Privacy Shield regime, is currently pending before the General Court and has been suspended in light of *Schrems II*.

217 Joined Cases C-203/15 and C-698/15, *Tele2 Sverige*, EU:C:2016:970.

218 *Digital Rights Ireland*, para 27.

219 *Tele2 Sverige*, para 99.

220 *Tele2 Sverige*, para 100.

221 *Tele2 Sverige*, para 103.

purposes, which it considered justified under the condition that it would be limited to 'what is strictly necessary'.[222]

The *Schrems* case is renowned for leading to the invalidation of the Safe Harbour Framework set out in Commission Decision 2000/520/EC that allowed the transfer of data to the US.[223] Reiterating the risks identified in *Digital Rights Ireland*, the Court underlined that any EU legislation that interfered with the fundamental rights of privacy and data protection enshrined in the Charter must 'lay down clear and precise rules governing the scope and application of a measure and imposing minimum safeguards, so that the persons whose personal data is concerned have sufficient guarantees enabling their data to be effectively protected against the risk of abuse and against any unlawful access and use of that data', while it also affirmed that the need for such guarantees is 'all the greater where personal data is subjected to automatic processing and where there is a significant risk of unlawful access to that data'.[224] The CJEU also found that legislation fails to be 'limited to what is strictly necessary' in those cases where 'it authorises, on a generalised basis, storage of all the personal data of all the persons whose data has been transferred from the European Union to the United States without any differentiation, limitation or exception being made in the light of the objective pursued and without an objective criterion being laid down by which to determine the limits of the access of the public authorities to the data, and of its subsequent use, for purposes which are specific, strictly restricted and capable of justifying the interference which both access to that data and its use entail'.[225] The Court concluded that this constitutes an interference with the right to privacy.[226] It further noted the importance of effective legal remedies by noting that when legislation fails to provide for any option to seek legal remedies in order to enforce the data subject's right to access, to rectification or to erasure, then it 'does not respect the essence of the fundamental right to effective judicial protection, as enshrined in Article 47 of the Charter'.[227]

---

222 *Tele2 Sverige*, para 108. In doing so, the CJEU built on its previous reasoning in *Digital Rights*, paras 51ff.

223 Commission Decision of 26 July 2000 pursuant to Directive 95/46/EC on the adequacy of the protection provided by the safe harbour privacy principles and related frequently asked questions issued by the US Department of Commerce [2000] OJ L 215/7.

224 *Schrems*, para 91.

225 *Schrems*, para 93.

226 *Schrems*, para 94.

227 *Schrems*, para 95.

8 *Principles Related to Criminal Procedure*

In general, criminal procedure shares the distinct nature attributed to criminal law in democratic societies: on the one hand, *it functions in the direction of protecting legal interests against crime*, being the mechanism through which criminal offences are adjudicated and criminal penalties are imposed (i.e. the most onerous among the sanctions that the State applies); on the other hand, *it guarantees the personal freedoms of individuals* by prohibiting arbitrariness on behalf of the State when exercising its punitive powers in the field of criminal justice. Consequently, insofar as criminal procedure is considered to be materialising fundamental constitutional guarantees that confirm the democratic character of a State, it is governed by legal principles of equivalent significance.[228]

That said, it is fair to argue that, apart from safeguards deriving from data protection rules, *the fundamental principles of criminal procedure enshrined in EU primary and secondary law* undeniably apply when data collected through the EU information systems is used in the context of criminal proceedings. In this respect, articles 47 (on the guarantees related to a fair trial) and 48 (on the rights of the defence) of the Charter are of central importance at the EU level, along with the Directives adopted based on article 82(2)(b) TFEU to approximate national provisions on the rights of persons involved in criminal proceedings. Among those, for example, *the presumption of innocence* (which is particularly relevant to the conditions and the consequences of considering an individual to be a 'suspect') is recognised by Directive (EU) 2016/343 as applying at all stages of the criminal proceedings after a person is 'suspected or accused of having committed a criminal offence';[229] thus, judicial authorities are bound by the obligations stemming from the presumption of innocence when presented with information provided by the systems in the context of criminal proceedings, just as when assessing any other type of evidence included in a case file.

However, in spite of this apparent conclusion, evidence based on information systems may sometimes cause *implications*, especially where procedural measures involving sensitive data are normally linked to *special guarantees*. Most notably, there are several aspects of using DNA data in criminal

---

228 Claus Roxin and Bernd Schünemann, *Strafverfahrensrecht* (29th edn, Beck 2017) 9; Adam Papadamakis, *Criminal Procedure* [in Greek] (8th edn, Sakkoulas 2018) 4–6; Nikolaos Androulakis, *Fundamental Principles of Criminal Procedure Law* [in Greek] (4th, PN Sakkoulas 2012) 14–19; Theocharis Dalakouras, *Criminal Procedure Law—Volume 1* [in Greek] (PN Sakkoulas 2012) 13; Aggelos Konstantinidis, *Criminal Procedure Law—Basic concepts* [in Greek] (Sakkoulas 2014) 2–6.

229 Art 2 of the Directive.

proceedings that are rightfully criticised as being problematic in terms of respecting fundamental law principles, most importantly the principle of proportionality, or even the primary obligation not to violate human dignity. These critical aspects have indicatively given rise to questions such as whether DNA data can be collected for any criminal offence or just criminal offences of a minimum gravity; whether it may be stored to process it with regard to criminal offences already committed or future criminal activities as well; whether it may come just from data subjects found guilty or even from ones acquitted (or from persons not suspected at all); whether it should be possible to use force to obtain it (thus violating human dignity according to the criticism expressed) or only less intrusive means, etc.[230] As a result, certain legal orders in the EU allow for related evidence to be acquired and evoked in criminal proceedings only under specific conditions; in fact, DNA data is collected, stored and processed under quite varying conditions in each Member State. For instance, according to the Greek Code of Criminal Procedure (article 201), it is possible to obtain a DNA sample *only if there are serious indications that a person has committed a felony or a misdemeanour punishable with a penalty of at least one year of imprisonment*, due to restrictions emanating from the presumption of innocence and the principle of proportionality.[231] Clearly, when such key prerequisites exist, it should be required for them to be met in all cases of similar characteristics within the context of a single legal order. In view of the above, the provision of article 3 (and the equivalent one of article 4) *of the Prüm Decision*, that, when an automated search in the national DNA databases returns a match, 'the national contact point of the searching Member State shall receive in an automated way the reference data with which a match has been found', means that authorities in a Member State where special conditions apply with regard to obtaining DNA data may automatically reach DNA data that was collected in another Member State, even if the latter applies lesser standards of guarantees.[232] As interconnecting the national databases of the Member States has drastically evolved in the last few years, while the EU refers to national legislations or insufficient non-EU legal instruments for guarantees,[233] the direct use of DNA data obtained through the

230 See extended analysis of the problems and further references in Symeonidou-Kastanidou in *DNA analysis* 3ff.

231 Theocharis Dalakouras, 'The Principle of Proportionality and procedural coercive measures' [in Greek] [2005] Poinika Chronika 961, 966; Konstantinidis 271ff.

232 Kaiafa-Gbandi, 'Information exchange' 151–152.

233 See above, section 7.3, regarding the non-application of Directive (EU) 2016/680. In reality the Prüm framework has never functioned under an EU data protection regime: at first, Directive 95/46/EC of 24 October 1995 on the protection of individuals with regard to the

Prüm framework as evidence in criminal proceedings *is a potential threat for procedural safeguards* in those legal orders that provide for special requirements with regard to collecting such data. Indeed, the structure of the Prüm framework in essence ensures solely the application of the lowest common denominator of the relevant guarantees existing in the Member States.

Furthermore, a distinct aspect of the discussion on the rules of criminal procedure that apply when data obtained through the EU information systems is used in the context of criminal proceedings relates to the issue of criminalising *neutral acts*.[234] In this case, fundamental rights are affected not just by the said criminalisation and the imposition of penalties for the respective criminal offences, which extend the restrictions on the personal liberty of individuals in a disputed manner, but also by the relative expansion of investigative measures of criminal procedure that are questioned even as to their respect for human dignity (i.e. obtaining DNA samples by force).[235] More specifically, in relation to such an offence (e.g. '*receiving training*' in the form of 'taking flying lessons'[236] for the purpose of committing a terrorist offence in the future), evidence concerning the act of the accused/defendant must be supplemented with evidence substantiating his or her criminal intentions. Thus, the evidence must cover not only the intent to commit the said act (of training), but also the

processing of personal data and on the free movement of such data [1995] OJ L 281/31 stated in art 3 that it 'shall not apply to the processing of personal data:—in the course of an activity which falls outside the scope of Community law, such as (...) the activities of the State in areas of criminal law'; subsequently, Framework Decision 2008/977/JHA, which did cover EU criminal law, did not apply to acts adopted prior to its entry into force (art 28); and, as already, mentioned, a similar provision exists in Directive (EU) 2016/680 as well.

234 Sieber in *Alternative Systems* 6 refers to them as 'temporarily early (often everyday) preparatory activities that are performed with ultimately criminal intentions'.

235 A similar situation, that has given rise to criticism and a relatively recent legislative reform, has occurred in the USA. Under US law, searches and seizures are covered by the Fourth Amendment ('the right of the people to be secure in their persons, houses, papers, and effects, against unreasonable searches and seizures, shall not be violated, and no Warrants shall issue, but upon probable cause, supported by Oath or affirmation, and particularly describing the place to be searched, and the persons or things to be seized'). Surveillance is a form of search; in 2001, aiming to prevent and combat terrorism, and in response to the 9/11 hits, the US government adopted the Patriot Act, which drastically affected *surveillance* procedures. On the basis of this evolution, law enforcement authorities were allowed to access electronic evidence by obtaining a basic search warrant instead of a surveillance warrant, which requires higher evidentiary showing. What is more, the Act permitted the use of 'sneak-and-peak' warrants (ie a warrant which law enforcement can delay notifying to the person affected).

236 The example is used in Explanatory Report to the Additional Protocol to the Council of Europe Convention on the Prevention of Terrorism of 22.10.2015 (para 41).

aim to commit another criminal offence (in this example a terrorist offence) in the future. However, since it is not necessary for the individual to have already initiated the commission of the future criminal offence or even for it to be perceivable to take place in the imminent future, there may be very little evidence *objectively* indicating the individual's aim to commit it. Consequently, a relevant investigation may probably need to have an *unusually wide scope* and include almost any information on a person's associations, daily activities, travelling, etc., i.e. information that appears to have no relevance to *criminal* activity, so as to be able to reveal any hint of this person's future plans.[237]

Thus, opening the scope of investigation in a manner that does not leave much information out of the collection process is another factor that may challenge fundamental principles of procedural law.[238] In this respect, and given that exceptionally intrusive and ambiguous investigating measures are often justified with regard to serious criminal offences,[239] like terrorist offences, a point of concern arises in reference to the fact that the newly established criminal offences that involve neutral acts, like the ones covered by 'receiving training', and place the latter acts within the framework of anti-terrorism legislation, allow for the controversial measures of criminal procedure to be used at such early stages of criminal behaviour.[240]

However, any grave violations of fundamental rights and guarantees cannot be tolerated in the context of the EU judicial cooperation in criminal matters. This is not only due to *the binding force of the Charter*, but also in view of certain *recent legislative and case-law developments, mainly with regard to EU mutual recognition instruments*. It is now well established that EU judicial cooperation in criminal matters, founded on a *presumed* notion of 'mutual trust' between the judicial systems of the Member States, for many years evolved in an uneven manner, i.e. by promoting drastic operational instruments on the one side, without instituting effective remedies for the individuals involved on the other, which in essence amounted to perceiving respect for fundamental rights as a given. Criticism was intense throughout these developments,[241] while national

237 See also on this Kaiafa-Gbandi, 'Information exchange' 150–151.

238 See the types of data stored by Europol (under section 2.1) as an example of collecting almost any type of information that could perhaps reveal a criminal connection or intent, as well of collecting it in a manner that could not be considered to provide in itself for acceptable evidence in all cases.

239 According to Symeonidou-Kastanidou in *DNA analysis* 10f, the measure could indeed be justified for offences of serious gravity, already committed (ie not a future offence) along with specific indications of guilt.

240 Sieber in *Alternative Systems* 7.

241 European Criminal Policy Initiative, 'A Manifesto on European Criminal Procedure' [2013] ZIS 430; Valsamis Mitsilegas, 'The Constitutional Implications of Mutual Recognition in

legislators[242] and national courts[243] 'questioned' this presumption of mutual trust by adding to their respective national legislation, or by applying in practice, grounds for refusal to execute EU legal instruments that did not exist in EU law, hence, violating their obligations deriving from the specific EU legal framework.

Against this background, EU institutional change has been rather delayed and comparatively slow. Such change was dictated primarily *by the problematic application of the European arrest warrant*,[244] which, at the EU level, was initially acknowledged by the European Commission and the European

---

Criminal Matters in the EU' [2006] Common Market Law Review 1277, and 'Constitutional Principles of the European Community and European Criminal Law' [2007] European Journal of Law Reform 301, 312; Maria Kaiafa-Gbandi, 'Case-law of the European Court of Justice and the new possibilities for EU intervention to the criminal law of Member States' [in Greek] [2006] Poiniki Dikaiosyni 476, 478, and 'Current developments of criminal law in the EU and Rule of Law deficiencies' [in Greek] [2006] Poinika Chronika 577, 587–589; Ester Herlin-Karnell, *The Constitutional Dimension of European Criminal Law* (Hart Publishing 2012) 24–25; Alicia Hinarejos, 'The Lisbon Treaty Versus Standing Still: A View from the Third Pillar' [2009] European Constitutional Law Review 99, 101–102; Estella Baker and Christopher Harding, From past imperfect to future perfect? A longitudinal study of the Third Pillar [2009] European Law Review 25, 40; Olga Tsolka, 'Mutual recognition of criminal judicial decisions and protection of fundamental rights in the "area of freedom, security and justice" of the EU' [in Greek] [2018] Poinika Chronika 425; Stefanos Pavlou, 'The European Union and the ECHR' [in Greek] [2008] Poinika Chronika 97; Christos Mylonopoulos, 'Community Criminal Law and General Principles of Community Criminal Law' [in Greek] [2010] Poinika Chronika 161, 162–164; Grigoris Kalfelis, 'Extraditing Greek Citizens' [in Greek] [2007] Poiniki Dikaiosyni 1188.

242 See eg UK's 'Extradition Act 2003', which in 2014 was amended to make a violation of the principle of proportionality ground to refuse execution of a European arrest warrant; section 21A(4): 'The judge must order D's discharge if the judge makes one or both of these decisions (a) that the extradition would not be compatible with the Convention rights; (b) that the extradition would be disproportionate'. See Valsamis Mitsilegas, *EU Criminal Law after Lisbon* (Hart Publishing 2016) 145f.

243 For example, although the European Parliament in its 'Report of 28 January 2014 PE 522.805v04-00, A7-0039/2014 with recommendations to the Commission on the review of the European Arrest Warrant' (2013/2109(INL)) called national authorities to examine the principle of proportionality *before issuing* a European arrest warrant (not as ground for refusal to execute), a Greek court refused to execute a European arrest warrant *invoking the Parliament's Report*, in a case where it considered that an execution would entail serious problems from a fundamental principles of criminal law perspective [Judicial Council of Appeals of Athens (Criminal law section) 1/2016, NOMOS database].

244 See a concise systemisation and evaluation of the CJEU case-law dealing with the respective problems in Maria Kaiafa-Gbandi, 'CJEU case law and the European Arrest Warrant: Fundamental directions and contemporary trends (Part B)' [in Greek] [2019] Poiniki Dikaiosyni 153; also European Criminal Policy Initiative 430ff. Extensively on the European arrest warrant Libor Klimek, *European Arrest Warrant* (Springer 2014).

Parliament;[245] in addition, and quite significantly, it was also ascertained by the European Court of Human Rights (ECtHR).[246] Owing to this evolution, and as the EU had already been legislating in the field of procedural rights based on article 82(2)(c) TFEU (supplementing its past mutual recognition instruments), *breaches* in the EU approach to irrefutably assume the existence of 'blind' mutual trust *gradually appeared.*[247]

In particular, from a secondary EU law perspective, the latest mutual recognition instruments contain clauses for *'refusal to execute'* under certain conditions, when there is proof that the fundamental rights of the persons involved are not adequately respected. From a case-law perspective, the CJEU, following similar positions it had previously expressed in the field of *EU asylum law*,[248] accepted that, even when not explicitly provided for, serious fundamental rights violations or core problems in the national judicial system of a Member State can give rise to refusal to execute a European arrest warrant.[249] Although limited in scope and demanding with regard to the threshold of violations or systemic problems to be ascertained for the unwritten grounds

245 See Council, 'Revised version of the European handbook on how to issue a European Arrest Warrant' 17195/1/10 (that was the second version of the Handbook, which was subsequently revised in 2017); Commission 'Report on the implementation since 2007 of the Framework Decision of 13 June 2002 on the European arrest warrant and the surrender procedures between Member States' COM (2011) 175; European Parliament Report PE 522.805v04-00, A7-0039/2014 (2013/2109(INL)); also Marta Bargis, 'Personal Freedom and Surrender' in *Handbook criminal procedure* 339–348, Mitsilegas, *EU Criminal Law after Lisbon* 142–146 and Klimek 323–338.

246 Mitsilegas, *EU Criminal Law after Lisbon* 129ff; Tsolka, 'Mutual recognition' 425ff; Giacomo Biagioni, 'Avotinš v. Latvia—The Uneasy Balance Between Mutual Recognition of Judgments and Protection of Fundamental Rights' [2016] European Papers 579; Caroline Morgan, 'The European Arrest Warrant and Defendants' Rights: An Overview' in Rob Blekxton and Wooter van Ballegooij (eds), *Handbook on the European Arrest Warrant* (Asser Press 2005) 205 ff.

247 See on this Valsamis Mitsilegas, 'The European Model of Judicial Cooperation in Criminal Matters: Towards Effectiveness based on Earned Trust' [2019] Rev. Bras. de Direito Processual Penal 565.

248 See Mitsilegas in *EU Criminal Law after Lisbon* 136ff, and in 'The European Model of Judicial Cooperation in Criminal Matters' 575.

249 See Case C-399/11 *Stefano Melloni v Ministerio Fiscal* EU:C:2013:107, para 63, but then, departing from it, Joined Cases C-404/15 and C-659/15 PPU *Aranyosi and Căldăraru* EU:C:2016:198, paras 88, 92, 93, Case C-216/18 PPU *LM* EU:C:2018:586, para 72ff, Case C-220/18 PPU *ML* EU:C:2018:589, para 117. See Maria Kaiafa-Gbandi, 'CJEU case law' (Part A) and (Part B) 1ff and 153ff respectively; Sergio Carrera and Valsamis Mitsilegas, *Upholding the Rule of Law by scrutinising judicial independence-The Irish Court's request for a preliminary ruling on the European Arrest Warrant* (CEPS 2018); Mitsilegas, 'The European Model of Judicial Cooperation in Criminal Matters' 578–585.

of refusal to function, this divergence from the older CJEU position to consider respect for fundamental rights indisputably presumed within the EU is considered to be a key development.[250]

Most significantly, this new direction is also supported by the provisions of the Directive on the *European Investigation Order* (EIO), which currently regulates the field of Member States obtaining *evidence* through measures carried out in other Member States. According to the Directive, a national authority may issue an EIO only when considering it 'necessary and proportionate' for the purpose of the respective proceedings 'taking into account the rights of the suspected or accused person' and for measures that 'could have been ordered under the same conditions in a similar domestic case'.[251] Likewise, the executing authority may not recognise or execute the EIO, in cases where its execution is incompatible with its obligations under article 6 TEU and the Charter, or when the EIO concerns an investigative measure restricted under its law to a category of offences or to offences punishable by a certain threshold, which does not include the offence covered by the EIO.[252]

Under the light of these provisions directly concerning evidence, which are also important from the perspective of moving away from the original stance to *presume* that EU criminal law instruments as a rule do not violate

250 See Mitsilegas in *EU Criminal Law after Lisbon* 139; also in 'The European Model of Judicial Cooperation in Criminal Matters' 582f, for questions left unanswered by the CJEU's ruling in the Aranyosi case.

251 Art 6(1) of Directive 2014/41/EU.

252 Art 11(1)(f),(h) of Directive 2014/41/EU. See on this Rosanna Belfiore, 'European Investigation Order in Criminal Matters: Developments in Evidence gathering across Europe' [2015] EuCLR 316; Silvia Allegrezza, 'Collecting criminal evidence across the European Union: the European Investigation Order between flexibility and proportionality' in Stefano Ruggeri (ed), *Transnational evidence and multicultural inquiries in Europe* (Springer 2014) 51ff; Regina Garcimartín Montero, 'The European Investigation Order and the Respect for Fundamental Rights in Criminal Investigations' [2017] Eucrim 45; Lorena Bachmaier, 'Towards the Transposition of Directive 2014/41 regarding the European Investigation Order in Criminal Matters' [2015] Eucrim 47; Mitsilegas, 'The European Model of Judicial Cooperation in Criminal Matters' 573; Frank Zimmermann, Sanja Glaser and Andreas Motz, 'Mutual recognition and its Implications for the Gathering of Evidence in Criminal proceedings: a Critical Analysis of the Initiative for a European Investigation Order' [2011] EuCLR 56; Aristomenis Tzanetis, 'The European Investigation Order (incorporating Directive 2014/41/EU by Law 4489/2017)' [in Greek] [2018] Poinika Chronika 81; Stamatis Daskalopoulos, 'European Investigation Order (EIO): The new Institution of Judicial Cooperation in Criminal Matters in the European Union' [in Greek] [2018] Poinika Chronika 173. See also in comparison to the European Evidence Warrant Marcello Daniele and Ersilia Calvanese, 'Evidence Gathering' in *Handbook criminal procedure* 354ff.

fundamental rights,[253] it is fair to argue that national courts should strive to make use of any margin provided by EU law and case-law for them to examine the legality of evidence deriving from EU information systems, in the sense that such legality should not be automatically assumed just because the data is collected or exchanged in accordance with the legal acts governing the function of the systems. This could be particularly relevant to DNA data, with regard to which unconditional collection in some Member States is considered to violate human dignity, which is of course protected under the EU Charter. In this regard, clauses of the EIO or even a method similar to the procedure introduced by the CJEU (i.e. asking for clarifications on specific fundamental rights issues) should be utilised where possible.[254]

Problems like the ones mentioned above could become increasingly relevant, especially if the criminalisation of neutral acts continues to be employed as a method to prevent serious crime from occurring; however, it should be stressed that, at the same time, the latter is an issue of central importance also with regard to the very actions of law enforcement (namely *police*) authorities themselves, as will be demonstrated and discussed under the following section.

9 *Principles and Rights Related to the Precognitive Paradigm of Criminal Law*

9.1 The EU Information Systems and the Emerging *Precognitive* Paradigm of Criminal Law

As has been established above, there is a stable, consistent and multifold connection between the information systems examined and criminal law purposes, within a broader setting of what seems to be a new law enforcement paradigm.[255] This paradigm manifests itself mostly through the direct involvement of law enforcement in gathering and processing data, namely in the context of law enforcement surveillance practices,[256] but is also served by subjecting information systems to primary or secondary criminal purposes, as

253 Mitsilegas, *EU Criminal Law after Lisbon* 130, and 'The European Model of Judicial Cooperation in Criminal Matters' 581f.

254 See on this also Daniele and Calvanese 378ff. Collecting DNA samples is regulated by the Prüm Decision (up to a point) and then by national laws of the Member States. The recent development of the Prüm framework may render the issuing of a EIO less preferable than searching the databases of other Member States; however, the abovementioned arguments also apply to any type of evidence that would be unacceptable in the context of a national legal order, eg a statement provided by an accused person testifying as a witness.

255 Bachmaier in *Alternative Systems* 171–172.

256 Bachmaier in *Alternative Systems* 171–172.

the EU has focused on internal security as one of the primary goals within the area of freedom, security and justice. This is also consistent with a broader paradigm shift in the function of surveillance under criminal law, as surveillance methods are increasingly used in order to *prevent* crime and not mainly during the stage of *detecting, investigating, prosecuting* committed crimes or *punishing* their perpetrators after the fact, as was the rule in earlier crime control models of the previous century.[257]

This field of law enforcement activity effectively falls under the broader aims of preventive criminal law. We have already seen the emergence of a distinct criminal law field of criminalising prima facie neutral acts, such as traveling, when this is done for terrorist purposes, according to article 9 of Directive (EU) 2017/541 on combating terrorism, which has been described as a new *pre-preventive* stage in criminal law.[258] The new field under examination here, which takes place before the pre-preventive stage and extends beyond criminalising and punishing to broader surveillance and data processing for the purposes of combating crime, and which mainly relies on expanded law enforcement surveillance activity and consists effectively of *an extended pre-preventive* stage, could be described as a *precognitive* paradigm of criminal law.

In the context of this *precognitive* paradigm, it seems that the bulk of law enforcement activities under the new criminal law approach is transferred to this *extended pre-preventive* stage of countering crime. '*Precognitive*' seems an appropriate term to describe it, since this stage of criminal justice mainly consists of data gathering and analysis activity, with the focus being on identifying potential links with criminal activity, a process which is set to be undertaken *at a later stage in the future*. In other words, data is processed at this point in order to function as a *pro-gnosis* or *pre-knowledge* of information which might later be deemed as important with regard to criminal activities and because it is *predicted* that it might be useful in the future.

In that sense, the data gathered creates a wide circle of knowledge or potential knowledge by law enforcement authorities of various facts or indications, even though this knowledge might not yet be connected to a crime. Then, when a link with a specific criminal activity appears, this *pre-knowledge* can

257 See more generally on this note, Maria Kaiafa-Gbandi, 'Surveillance models in the security state and fairness of criminal trial' in Maria Kaiafa-Gbandi and Cornelius Prittwitz (eds), *Surveillance and criminal repression in contemporary anti-crime policy* [in Greek] (Nomiki Bibliothiki 2011) 63–98.

258 See also on this point, Kaiafa-Gbandi, 'Information exchange' 171. See on a similar analysis with regard to Framework Decision 2008/919/JHA on combating terrorism, Maria Kaiafa-Gbandi, 'Preventing terrorism and the new pre-preventive criminal law: new crimes for combating crime in the EU' [in Greek] [2009] Poinika Chronika 385, 397–400.

suddenly become useful, as it can provide law enforcement with pieces of the puzzle that can help fill out the broader picture of a crime. To venture a more concise definition, the *precognitive* paradigm of criminal law is the one taking place long before the traditional criminal trial, pre-trial and preventive stages of the criminal justice mechanism, at a stage where information gathering and analysis is elevated to the main objective of law enforcement authorities' activity, in order to accumulate knowledge, even when this knowledge is not linked to a particular crime or suspect yet, that could be potentially relevant at a later stage. In the era of surveillance and big data, this *precognitive* law enforcement activity that is meant to serve criminal law purposes seems to gradually extend its reach—for instance, by expanding the scope of non-law enforcement EU information systems to cover law enforcement purposes, as has been noted above—and become an essential part of the contemporary anti-crime approach across EU Member States and beyond. In this context, the EU information systems examined here *from the perspective of criminal law* serve a pivotal role in this *precognitive* paradigm. As it breaks out of the traditional confines of criminal law and law enforcement, the concept of this *precognitive* paradigm warrants the following further analysis in order to delineate its scope and content.

It is well-established that criminal justice mechanisms can legitimately—and within certain boundaries—intrude on the rights and liberties of individuals in order to *combat* crime, i.e. investigate, prosecute and punish crimes. The most common occurrences in the context of law enforcement are legitimate infringements on personal liberty, the right to one's private life, the right to property, etc. Similar powers are awarded to law enforcement in order to prevent crime. However, at the preventive stage, where no crime has been committed yet, these powers are subject to more limitations and allowed to a less intrusive extent.

Under the new *pre-preventive* approach effectively endorsed by the EU, the exception becomes the norm and these intrusive powers of law enforcement authorities are elevated to include a broader scope by taking place even before the *preventive* stage.[259] This is evident, first of all, in how criminal law provisions are construed. New criminal law provisions begin to emerge which deviate from the rule that a *harmful act* is to be found at the core of a definition of a crime, i.e. an act that inflicts harm to or at the very least places a legal interest

259 See also Bachmaier in *Alternative Systems* 172–173, who elaborates in the context of terrorist offences.

in endangerment, according to the Rechtsgut theory of German criminal law,[260] which has influenced many other jurisdictions, Greece included,[261] or the harm principle, widely embraced by common-law jurisdictions.[262] Instead, provisions like the new offence of travelling abroad for the purpose of terrorism, which EU Member States are obliged to criminalise according to article 9 of Directive (EU) 2017/541 on combating terrorism,[263] criminalise prima facie neutral acts, shifting the focus on the individual's *intentions* and state of mind.[264]

Against this setting of a new *pre-preventive* approach in criminal law enforcement and of pushing crime control to a previous stage of neutral acts in order to serve crime *prevention*, *information* emerges as a contender for the fundamental role of *evidence* as the basis for applying criminal justice. In this context, information that is merely indicative is perceived as necessary and

---

260 Hans-Heinrich Jescheck and Thomas Weigend, *Lehrbuch des Strafrechts: Allhemeiner Teil* (Duncker & Humblot 1996) 104–105; Roland Hefendehl, Andrew von Hirsch and Wolfgang Wohlers, *Die Die Rechtsgutstheorie: Legitimationsbasis des Strafrechts oder dogmatisches Glasperlenspiel?* (Nomos 2003); Claus Roxin, *Strafrecht Allgemeiner Teil Bd. 1* (C H Beck 2005) 11ff; Markus Dubber, 'Theories of Crime and Punishment in German Criminal Law' [2006] The American Journal of Comparative Law 679.

261 Ioannis Manoledakis, *The legal interest as a fundamental concept of criminal law* [in Greek] (Sakkoulas 1998).

262 Albin Eser, 'The Principle of "Harm" in the Crime Concept: A Comparative Analysis of the Criminally Protected Legal Interests' [1996] Duquesne University Law Review 345; Joel Feinberg, *The Moral Limits of the Criminal Law (Oxford: Oxford University Press): Harm to Others (1984); Offense to Others (1985); Harm to Self (1986); Harmless Wrongdoing (1988)*; RA Duff 'Harms and Wrongs' (2001) Buffalo Criminal Law Review 13; Andrew von Hirsch, 'Der Rechtsgutsbegriff und das "Harm Principle"' [2002] Goltdammer's Archiv für Strafrecht 2; Andrew Ashworth, *Principles of Criminal Law* (OUP 2006) 30–39; Douglas Husak, *Overcriminalization: The Limits of the Criminal Law* (Oxford University Press 2008) 65–72; A P Simester and Andrew von Hirsch, *Crimes, Harms, and Wrong* (Hart Publishing 2011) 35–88; Tatjana Hörnle, '"Rights of Others" in Criminalisation Theory' in A P Simester, Antje du Bois-Pedain and Ulfrid Neumann (eds), *Liberal Criminal Law Theory, Essays for Andreas von Hirsch* (Hart Publishing 2014) (*Liberal Criminal Law*) 169ff; Winfried Hassemer, 'The Harm Principle and the Protection of 'Legal Goods' (Rechtsgüterschutz): a German Perspective' in *Liberal Criminal Law* 187ff; RA Duff and Sandra Marshall, '"Remote Harms" and the Two Harm Principles' in *Liberal Criminal Law* 205ff; Nina Peršak 'Using "Quality of Life" to Legitimate Criminal Law Intervention: Gauging Gravity, Defining Disorder' in *Liberal Criminal Law* 225ff.

263 A similar recommendation for UN members is included under paragraph 6 of UN Security Council Resolution 2178/2014 <www.un.org/securitycouncil/s/res/2178-(2014)> accessed 3 February 2020.

264 See analysis of this point in Mitsilegas, 'European Criminal Law and the Dangerous Citizen' 739–743; Kaiafa-Gbandi, 'Information exchange' 151; Niovi Vavoula, 'Prevention, Surveillance, and the Transformation of Citizenship in the "Security Union": The Case of Foreign Terrorist Fighters' [2018] Queen Mary School of Law Legal Studies Research Paper No. 293/2018.

sufficient in and of itself in order to shed light on an individual's state of mind, upon which criminalisation now rests.[265]

This emphasis on information is the bedrock of the *precognitive* paradigm, as data is declared the new central tool in law enforcement. It is also closely connected to another pivotal concern, which becomes particularly troubling in the context of criminal law, namely the way that data is collected, stored and processed. As the above analysis of the information systems demonstrates, they collect massive amounts of data in a manner that does not necessarily *discriminate* between individuals who are justifiably deemed to be of interest with regard to crimes and those who are unrelated. The case of PNR data is perhaps the most obvious example of this evolution from collecting and processing data related to *specific* crimes and connected to *specific* individuals who are *of interest* to these crimes, to mass collection of data that is *not directly related to any crime*, collected from *unrelated* data subjects, that could be used *if* a (potential or already committed) crime is identified *later* in the process. When it comes to PNR data, this is collected from *everyone* aboard a flight even when no potential criminal act has been discovered yet and includes personal information that is prima facie *unrelated* to the commission of crimes, like itinerary and contact details, travel status, baggage information, travel agent information, or even seat number and seat information of the passenger.

The element of '*mass collection*' is of outstanding importance.[266] On the one hand, it appears to *contradict* in an obvious manner (i.e. without conducting in depth analysis) and as a rule (i.e. in any case it is acknowledged to occur) key principles of the personal data protection regime (namely the principles of purpose limitation and of data minimisation), and to effectively *undermine* the criteria of necessity and proportionality. On the other hand, it has already been *disapproved* by the CJEU, when it was most notably used as an integral part of the reasoning supporting the annulment of the data retention Directive (where the CJEU referred to a 'vast quantity of data').[267] Although that Directive concerned the collection, storage and sharing of communications

265 Kaiafa-Gbandi, 'Information exchange' 169ff.

266 See especially Kaiafa-Gbandi, 'Information exchange' 171, introducing the concept of 'dual massiveness', i.e. massiveness as to both the data subjects affected and the persons involved in the collection and processing of the data, and stressing that 'massive and substantially unrestricted accumulation and use of information for citizens is attributed to illiberal regimes and erodes the foundations of democracy'.

267 Digital Rights Ireland, para 66; see above, section 7.2. See comments on the reasoning indicatively in Arianna Vedaschi and Valerio Lubello, 'Data Retention and its Implications

data, the EU legal framework presently regulating PNR data[268] is rightfully argued to bear *comparable* features.[269] Primarily, the core points made just above on the PNR Directive, i.e. regarding the lack of discrimination as to the subjects of the data collected and the absence of a link of the data to as much as a suspicion of a criminal offence, clearly correspond to the 'generalised manner' of collection and to the 'general absence of limits' highlighted by the CJEU in view of the annulment of the data retention Directive.[270] What is more, conclusions in the same direction can be drawn from the CJEU Opinion 1/2015 on the proposed PNR EU-Canada agreement.[271] There the CJEU held, among other findings, that the draft agreement's wording on the definition of a type of data, *also used in the PNR Directive*, 'cannot be regarded as being delimited with sufficient clarity and precision'; moreover, in examining the compatibility of the draft's retention periods with 'what is strictly necessary', it referred to a condition that *does not apply in the PNR Directive*.[272] Thus, and

for the Fundamental Right to Privacy; A European Perspective' [2015] Tilburg Law Review 14.

268 Mitsilegas, 'European Criminal Law and the Dangerous Citizen' 743, 746 refers to PNR data as 'key example' of 'pre-emptive mass surveillance'.

269 Criticism on 'mass' or 'bulk' collection of data or 'surveillance' interestingly involves three data collection regimes: communications data, *PNR data* and the financial data exchanged in the context of the anti-money laundering EU legislation. See this triplet in Tzanou 107ff, Mitsilegas, 'The Transformation of Privacy' 35ff, Kaiafa-Gbandi, 'Information exchange' 162.

270 Digital Rights Ireland, paras 56–60.

271 Opinion 1/15, pursuant to Article 218(11) TFEU, EU:C:2017:592.

272 See Opinion 1/15, paras 160 [regarding heading 17 of the draft, reading 'general remarks including Other Supplementary Information (OSI), Special Service Information (SSI) and Special Service Request (SSR) information', which the CJEU considered that 'it provides no indication as to the nature and scope of the information to be communicated, and it may even encompass information entirely unrelated to the purpose of the transfer of PNR data'; thus 'heading 17 does not set any limitation on the nature and scope of the information that could be set out thereunder (…) [and it] cannot be regarded as being delimited with sufficient clarity and precision'; *see a similar phrasing in the PNR Directive Annex I, point 12*] and 206f [regarding the draft connecting retention periods to the condition that 'in specific cases, objective evidence is identified from which it may be inferred that certain air passengers may present a risk in terms of the fight against terrorism and serious transnational crime even after their departure from Canada'; *such a condition is not included in the PNR Directive*] respectively; and for these observations see Vavoula 24–26.

in spite of the CJEU not stating it expressly,[273] 'mass collection' of data does exist at least in the example of PNR data.[274]

This essentially means that in this new *precognitive* paradigm of criminal law, not only are neutral acts brought into the scope of criminal law and law enforcement in the pre-preventive stage, based on the perpetrator's knowledge and/or intent, but also *neutral information is gathered* in the hopes of *being or potentially becoming useful* in the prevention, investigation and successful prosecution of such crimes. These two developments are in large part connected and derive from the same approach: as long as a definition of a crime can be primarily construed based on subjective elements that qualify an otherwise neutral act, so will neutral information emerge as necessary for identifying and delineating these subjective elements. In this context, the example of the *precognitive* approach to combating crime could also in part reflect a broader failure to construe criminal law provisions that are effective while adhering to the rule of law and criminal law principles.

In that sense, this approach forms the basis of what we can describe as the new *precognitive paradigm* of criminal law, where mass information gathering is conducted proactively by law enforcement authorities with the aim of *potentially* being useful for combatting crime. Even though at this stage of information gathering there may be no exercise of law enforcement in the traditional sense, as there may very well be no suspects or accused persons or even potential criminal acts at this point in time, it is evident from the above analysis that law enforcement authorities still exercise a function that is closely connected to their role of preventing or combating crime.

---

273 See comment on this in Mitsilegas, 'European Criminal Law and the Dangerous Citizen' 746, and further on Opinion 1/15 indicatively Christopher Kuner in 'International agreements, data protection, and EU fundamental rights on the international stage: Opinion 1/15 (EU-Canada PNR) of the Court of Justice of the EU' [2018] Common Market Law Review 857, and in 'Data Protection, Data Transfers, and International Agreements: the CJEU's Opinion 1/15' [2017] <https://verfassungsblog.de/data-protection-data-transfers-and-international-agreements-the-cjeus-opinion-115/> accessed 3 February 2020; Christopher Docksey, 'Opinion 1/15: Privacy and security, finding the balance' [2017] Maastricht Journal of European and Comparative Law 768; Elif Kuskonmaz and Elspeth Guild, 'EU exclusive jurisdiction on surveillance related to terrorism and serious transnational crime, case review on opinion 1/15 of the CJEU' [2018] European Law Review 583; Arianna Vedaschi and Chiara Graziani, 'PNR Agreements between Fundamental Rights and National Security: Opinion 1/15' [2018] <http://europeanlawblog.eu/2018/01/23/pnr-agreements-between-fundamental-rights-and-national-security-opinion-115/> accessed 3 February 2020.

274 The latest respective evolution, the interoperability scheme, is also strongly criticised for its impact on a *mass* collection of data; see Kaiafa-Gbandi, 'Information exchange' 171–173.

The fact that this function cannot be placed within the traditional framework of law enforcement raises concerns, as this means that from a criminal justice point of view there are no boundaries put in place to this activity. Even though there are certain rules, such as those examined earlier that relate to data protection (section 7) or criminal procedure (section 8) which can directly apply to this stage provided that the relevant requirements are met, one fundamental question remains: is it possible to also allow for some form of indirect or analogous application of important principles of criminal proceedings and fundamental rights of the accused or suspect in the context of criminal proceedings in this *precognitive* paradigm? These rights and principles must be examined to identify their underlying purpose and philosophy in order to determine whether they should in some form or degree be reflected and applied already in this *precognitive* law enforcement paradigm.

9.2 Law Enforcement Restrictions—the Principle of Proportionality

In general, the field of 'law enforcement'[275] activity is not regulated at an international level in the same manner and to the same extent as the field of criminal law and judicial cooperation. First of all, criminal law fundamental principles and guarantees have been widely agreed and consolidated in international conventions since the beginning of the second half of the twentieth century.[276] Similarly, international conventions have been subsequently adopted to ensure the criminalisation of certain harmful acts and to regulate judicial cooperation. Law enforcement activity, on the other hand, is traditionally equipped with powers which are less intrusive to the freedoms of the individuals (for example as to their duration) than criminal law measures and criminal penalties; moreover, it is accepted that law enforcement authorities are, and should be, granted certain leeway in their actions when dealing with risky situations, in order to be able to effectively fulfil their duty to avert

275 The term 'law enforcement' is used here in distinction to 'judicial' (see eg Prüm Decision preamble para 12 'The information obtained by comparing data should open up new investigative approaches for Member States and thus play a crucial role in assisting Member States' *law enforcement and judicial* authorities') and it involves the Police as well as any other authority with competence to prevent and investigate crime outside the framework of criminal proceedings (notwithstanding the fact that the same authorities can participate in criminal proceedings when provided by law).

276 Primarily, the ECHR (1950) in the context of the Council of Europe, as well as the ICCPR (1966) in the context of the UN guarantee the fundamental principles relating to criminal liability (arts 7 and 15 respectively) and to criminal procedure (arts 6 and 14 respectively); on the significance of these texts for the evolution of criminal law at an international level see Nikolaos Paraskevopoulos, *The foundations of criminal law—General Part: The criminal offence* [in Greek] (Sakkoulas 2008) 52ff.

dangers. And given that (especially) the police are not just responsible to prevent and combat crime, but also *to protect the public peace and order within a State*,[277] the rules on their functioning are basically constructed at *national* level. In accordance with these attributes, one can see that different competences have been conferred upon the EU in the area of judicial cooperation in criminal matters and in the framework of police cooperation.[278]

However, neither the absence of criminal law principles nor the differences spotted above entail that law enforcement activity is not governed by rules and limitations. On the contrary, the demand that a State's power to apply the law *by force* (which by definition includes law enforcement duties) must be delineated by principles and safeguards is an essential prerequisite for the democratic character of modern societies.[279] In addition, traditional police measures are perhaps indeed less intrusive than criminal law measures, but very often they serve crime *prevention*, meaning that they may be imposed in cases where no offence has been committed yet. Furthermore, it should be noted that international law *does* provide for some rules on the operation of law enforcement authorities. First of all, the UN introduced in 1979 the 'Code of Conduct for Law Enforcement Officials', which, among other obligations, recognises the law enforcement authorities' responsibility to 'respect and protect *human dignity* and maintain and uphold the human rights of all persons',[280] as well as to '*use force only when strictly necessary and to the extent required*

277 See Zoi Papaioannou, *Police law* [in Greek] (2nd edn, Sakkoulas 2005) 183, 188ff, and Presidential Decree 141/1991 art 93 for the Greek legal order; on the latter and especially on the dispute regarding its compatibility with the Greek Constitution see Elisavet Symeonidou-Kastanidou, 'Police violence: legislative framework and application issues' [in Greek] [2006] Nomiko Vima 1641 (where further references).

278 Judicial cooperation in criminal matters is based on the principle of mutual recognition of judicial decisions and the approximation of national legislations, which entail very drastic interventions in the national legal orders of the Member States, while police cooperation very much relies on information sharing and operational cooperation; compare art 82 (and 83) TFEU with art 87 (and 88) TFEU. See extensively on EU police cooperation Gaetano De Amicis, 'Horizontal Cooperation' in *Handbook criminal procedure* 250ff, as well as Synnøve Ugelvik, *Police Cooperation and Sovereignty in the EU: Norway's Lessons for Europe* (*Transnational Criminal Justice*) (Routledge 2019) 50–57 (and in various sections for interesting estimations from a national—the Norwegian—perspective).

279 Stergios Alexiadis, *Human Rights in Criminal Policy: twelve studies* [in Greek] (Sakkoulas 1990) 9–10.

280 Art 2 of the UN Code of Conduct for Law Enforcement Officials <www.ohchr.org/Documents/ProfessionalInterest/codeofconduct.pdf> accessed 3 February 2020 (see also 'Guidelines for the effective implementation of the Code of Conduct for Law Enforcement Officials' <www.coe.int/t/dg1/legalcooperation/economiccrime/cybercrime/cy%20activity%20Interface2006/un%20Guidelines%20CoC%20Law%20Enforcement%20Officers.pdf> accessed 3 February 2020.

for the performance of their duty'. Likewise, the 'Basic Principles on the Use of Force and Firearms by Law Enforcement Officials', adopted by the UN in 1990, also foster the '*strictly necessary*' criterion.[281]

In examining the Greek law with regard to the powers of the main domestic law enforcement authority (i.e. the Greek Police) as an *example* of national legislation, the following interesting points stand out. To begin with, the preventive duties of the police and the preventive acts that the police can perform are *enumerated* in law.[282] In this context, the principle of *necessity, as an aspect of the principle of proportionality*, is a key condition for the justification of several police measures, including searching persons, objects and areas that are not public or where access is not free.[283] Apart from necessity, a (general and depending on the officer's subjective assessment) *suspicion* regarding the commission of a criminal offence may become the justifying factor instead.[284] *Suspicion of criminal activity* also justifies checking a person's identity, even by force.[285] Legal scholars, on the other hand, argue that the latter should be allowed only in specific cases, where *concrete danger for an unidentified number of persons or objects ('common danger') arises*; similarly, that only *objective indications on the potential commission of a serious criminal offence* should justify body searches;[286] and, in any case, that, in order to effectively evaluate the necessity to apply police measures, it is imperative for the legislator to have *precisely defined the purpose that each measure shall*

---

281 See paras 15–16: '15. Law enforcement officials, *in their relations with persons in custody or detention*, shall not use *force, except when strictly necessary for the maintenance of security and order* within the institution, or when *personal safety is threatened*. 16. Law enforcement officials, in their relations with persons in custody or detention, shall not use *firearms*, except in self-*defence* or in the defence of others *against the immediate threat of death or serious injury*, or when *strictly necessary to prevent the escape* of a person in custody or detention *presenting the danger* referred to in principle 9' (<www.ohchr.org/Documents/ProfessionalInterest/firearms.pdf> accessed 3 February 2020). On these UN documents see Michael J. Trebilcock and Ronald J. Daniels, *Rule of Law Reform and Development: Charting the Fragile Path of Progress* (Edward Elgar Publishing 2008) 107–144.

282 Presidential Decree 141/1991 arts 93, 94 and 96 (ff).

283 See Presidential Decree 141/1991 art 96(3)(b), which refers to 'absolute necessity'.

284 See criticism in Symeonidou-Kastanidou, 'Police violence' 1641f.

285 Presidential Decree 141/1991 art 74(15)(g),(h). Regarding the concept of 'suspicion' see Nikolaos Livos, 'The procedural law position of those under suspicion to have committed a criminal offence' [in Greek] [1995] Poinika Chronika 1103.

286 See Symeonidou-Kastanidou, 'Police violence' 1643; cf. Athanasios Zachariadis, 'Preventive body searches, the principle of proportionality and the protection of human dignity' [in Greek] [1995] Yperaspisi 1237, 1241f.

serve.[287] In total, the notion that the more intrusive the measure, the more its prerequisites and the narrower its scope expresses the basic approach towards police activity and measures.[288] This is very important to note, because, corresponding to the *stricto sensu* assessment of the principle of proportionality, it takes into account the *impact* of a measure on the rights and freedoms of the person it concerns.

The central significance that the Greek legal order attributes to necessity and to the principle of proportionality as criteria for assessing law enforcement powers is in fact in line with the processes designed within the *immigration control EU information systems* to allow access for law enforcement purposes. As presented under section 2.2, the conditions that have to be met respectively have a clear reference to terms falling under the scope of the principle of proportionality, since the requested access must be *necessary for the purpose* of the prevention, detection or investigation of offences, *necessary and proportionate in a specific case*, and expected, based on *evidence or reasonable grounds*, to substantially contribute to the prevention, detection or investigation of the criminal offences in question.

Consequently, the fundamental rule that determines law enforcement obligations does exist at the EU level; it is *the principle of proportionality*, enshrined in EU primary law and case-law, which is thus governing the EU legislation *in the field of police cooperation* and *any law enforcement activity regulated by the EU*.[289] In view of the above, the principle of proportionality

287 Zachariadis 1243f.

288 Symeonidou-Kastanidou, 'Police violence' 1642; Zachariadis 1244; Nikolaos Androulakis, 'The limits of the investigative action and the principle of proportionality' [in Greek] [1975] Poinika Chronika 3, 9–11; Papaioannou 358; see also Adam Papadamakis, 'Issues concerning the Principle of Proportionality in Criminal proceedings' [in Greek] [2019] Poiniki Dikaiosyni 281; Georgios N. Triantafyllou, 'The Principle of Proportionality in Criminal Proceedings' [in Greek] [1990] Elliniki Dikaiosyni 301, 311 on the necessity of body searches in criminal proceedings; cf. Theocharis Dalakouras, *The Principle of Proportionality and procedural coercive measures* [in Greek] (Sakkoulas 1993) 224, on the intrusiveness of a measure compared to the gain for the procedure.

289 See Charter arts 5(4) TEU and 49(3) with regard to criminal law (concisely on the different aspects of the principle of proportionality in the EU see Mitsilegas, *EU Criminal Law after Lisbon* 43); and indicatively Kate Shaw, *The Court of Justice of the European Union: Subsidiary and Proportionality* (Brill Nijhoff 2018); Martin Böse, 'The Principle of Proportionality and the Protection of Legal Interests (Verhältnismäßigkeit und Rechtsgüterschutz)' [2011] EuCLR 35; Joanna Długosz 'The Principle of Proportionality in European Union Law as a Prerequisite for Penalization' [2017] Adam Mickiewicz University Law Review 283; Aharon Barack, *Proportionality Constitutional Rights and their Limitations* (Cambridge University Press 2012) 129ff; Giannakoula, *Crime and Sanctions* 366ff.

should be used to evaluate *all the procedures* established within the EU information systems (not just immigration control databases) granting access to the collected data for law enforcement purposes *as methods of 'police' search* (or search of any other law enforcement body that has the right to access the data) that may lead to action being taken against the subject of the data.

In this respect, it is of the utmost importance to ask two questions deriving from the principle of proportionality: (*a*) *whether there are any other, less intrusive measures that can be used instead*; (*b*) *how the impact on fundamental rights is weighed against the objectives pursued.* The first question corresponds to the notion of necessity and to the logical assumption that no measure can be deemed necessary, if another measure, less intrusive, can achieve the same results; in other words, no measure should be used as an end in itself. The second question relates to the *stricto sensu* assessment on proportionality conducted in the context of applying the criteria of the general version of the principle and aims to primarily exclude the setting of goals that are so 'ambitious' and demanding, that may by definition justify even the most intrusive amongst the measures that may be used to achieve them.[290]

To this end, *when viewing police access to information systems as a police investigation measure*, the following observations can be made, with relation to employing the principle of proportionality. First of all, in the cases of immigration control databases, in view of the issues identified just above, law enforcement purposes should remain distinct; in that sense, the choices made with regard to the types of data collected, the subjects concerned and the retention periods fixed should be made on the sole criterion of serving the purpose for which each system was designed (e.g. contributing to the handling of asylum applications, when it comes to Eurodac). To this extent, law enforcement rights should be subsequently determined by respecting the restrictions deriving from the conditions set in the previous stage of building the system's specific characteristics and by adopting even stricter rules where necessary and appropriate, e.g. as to the types of data stored in each system that can be processed for law enforcement purposes. Alternatively, if it is considered that law enforcement purposes should co-determine the very basic choices concerning the operation of the system (and result into a system like SIS, which has a dual purpose, for example), then this should be explicitly stated and *justified* and executed under the stricter conditions that such a project would have to satisfy. In other words, when law enforcement purposes affect the whole designing of an immigration control database, they should do it expressly; they should not

290 Petter Asp, 'Two Notions of Proportionality' in Kimmo Nuotio and Raimo Lahti (eds), *Festschrift in honour of Raimo Lahti* (University of Helsinki 2007) 207ff.

function as an *underlying* factor, because this would most likely push towards broadening the scope of the collection (or even loosening certain conditions, e.g. on retention periods etc., as it could be seen as an opportunity to collect as much data as possible and in more convenient terms) and, at the same time, it would 'disguise' the true purpose of these choices (e.g. of collecting any data going beyond what would be necessary for the immigration control objectives served by the specific system) and, thus, undermine the ability to check the respective rules against their true objective (i.e. law enforcement purposes) and by the corresponding criteria (namely the principle of proportionality). Therefore, requiring for immigration control aims to be distinct, clear and the only factor affecting the first stage of forming such a system in reality enhances the compatibility of the system with the principles governing law enforcement activity as well.

Furthermore, as far as the Prüm framework is concerned, given the sensitive nature of the data it mainly contains (DNA data) and the promoted access rights of law enforcement authorities across the EU, it seems appropriate to assume, in accordance with the arguments mentioned above with regard to criminal procedure, that any access granted to police authorities should as a minimum adhere to the same principles as access by judicial authorities, in those Member States where special conditions apply. Under this approach, access could be subject to approval by a judicial authority assigned by a Member State to review it, in the same way it is, for example, to be performed by the Greek authorities, where members of the judiciary will be placed 'on the spot' (at the Headquarters of the Greek Police) to take the necessary decisions immediately.[291]

Furthermore, it is clear that when purposes are very broadly defined, it is hard to assess whether data collection and processing is necessary to serve them. Most significantly, clear links to necessity are missing in the case of the blanket collection of PNR data. Contrary to the demands of necessity and of

---

291 On this evolution see <www.astynomia.gr/index.php?option=ozo_content&perform=view&id=50&Itemid=41&lang=EN>, accessed 3 February 2020: 'The Single Point Of Contact for the exchange of information on international police cooperation (SPOC) has been established as per Presidential Decree 178/2014, it will operate at a Section level on a 24 hours basis and it will be the contact point as regards cases of international police operational cooperation including all the enacted international and European communication focal points of the International Police Cooperation Division, in accordance with European models (EIXM) and best practices. The Single Point of Contact will be staffed with personnel of the Division's SIRENE, INTERPOL, and EUROPOL Sections (whose operational centers will be merged into it), and with officials of the Financial and Economic Crime Unit (S.D.O.E.), the Customs authorities and the Port Police/Hellenic Coast Guard, under the supervision of judicial and prosecutorial officials'.

specific purposes within the context of proportionality, PNR data appears to be collected today not for reasons related to flights (i.e. in relation to the security of a flight itself), but rather *on the occasion* of flights. In general, it would be possible to escalate the potential purposes for collecting data based on the intensity of their link to a particular air-travel, and thus the justification of their collection, as follows: first, the most intense justification would concern the aim of identifying persons who *intend to commit a criminal offence in the duration of the flight threatening its safety* (this requires collecting of data as part of the relevant *security* measures adopted, which notably involve checks on the persons travelling and their luggage). Then, one could think of the broader aim of identifying persons *who commit a criminal offence by taking the flight*, because e.g. they are absconding so as to avoid a pending arrest or they are using forged documents to travel or they are trying to illegally import/export objects (this also justifies having personal data available to the authorities prior to a flight and in relation to security checks). Following, nowadays one would have to think of the cases where *the very act of travelling by plane is a criminal offence in itself* (i.e. when travelling to commit terrorist offences or sexual offences against minors); although controversial in terms of substantive criminal law, because the acts criminalised do not *objectively* reveal any danger unless connected to a person's intent (thus requiring a much broader collection of data and also processing it after the flight), law enforcement authorities are justified to collect data related to the passengers and retain it for the purpose of investigating such criminal offences.[292] The collection of PNR data, though, goes beyond even the latter, as various types of data are stored and processed in order to perhaps reveal a link to a criminal offence not at all relevant to the flight in question.[293]

The most challenging, however, is without doubt the case of information collection and sharing conducted by Europol. To be concise, every aspect of this activity is of extreme character: the types of data collected and the persons it concerns (as presented in Part 1), Europol's access rights and the agencies it cooperates with, and, most intriguingly, the future perspectives of this activity, which include participating in the interoperability scheme and maintaining its priority to be 'the EU criminal information hub'.[294] Against current developments and the designed evolution, however, it should be clear at the EU

292 Based on the analysis in section 9.1, this amounts to functions of a pre-preventive criminal law.

293 Based on the analysis in section 9.1, this amounts to functions of a precognitive paradigm of criminal law.

294 Europol Programming Document 2019–2021 11f, 19, 41ff (<www.europol.europa.eu/publications-documents/europol-programming-document> accessed 3 February 2020);

level that Europol, being the 'European Union Agency for *Law Enforcement* Cooperation', should abide by *EU law enforcement principles*.

To this extent, it would be necessary to re-evaluate its architecture not (or at least not only) in relation to managing information from multiple sources (as already announced by Europol)[295] and to other operational 'challenges' and objectives, but mainly under the light of the principle of proportionality. More specifically, it would be important to form concrete categories of data depending on their degree of connection to criminal activity, and then define in accordance with these categories and their potential use the specific conditions for storing, processing and exchanging the data included in each category. This would not be foreign to the current institutional framework of Europol, which already appears to take into account the different characteristics of the subjects of the data and the different purposes served. However, the existing framework is clearly insufficient so far, due to the complex relative landscape, the extremely broad scope of the categories and their blurred limits, the equation of purposes of different gravity[296] and the adoption of wide exceptions with regard to procedural guarantees;[297] therefore, the principle of proportionality would dictate, for example, limiting the types and volume of data *exchanged with third countries* (which is a purpose of serious gravity) in a way that would exclude data feebly connected to criminal activity (such as means of communication or transport used, or 'behavioural data', which includes lifestyle, places frequented, etc.) when it concerns the possible commission of offences *in the future*.[298]

Moreover, in view of the possibility to use data collected by Europol in the context of criminal proceedings, *judicial oversight* over the respective procedures, that may ensure the legality of the collection and processing, is a demand already strongly supported. In 2000, the Council of Europe identified a distinction between States where police service is 'independent of the Public Prosecution, and enjoys considerable discretion' and other States where 'policing is supervised, or indeed directed, by the public prosecutor'. In view

Europol Strategy 2016–2020 11 (<www.europol.europa.eu/publications-documents/europol-strategy-2016-2020> accessed 3 February 2020).

295 Europol Strategy 2016–2020 11.

296 See for example the introductory phrase in Europol Regulation Annex II.B.

297 See for example Europol Regulation art 25(5).

298 On the subject of sharing Europol data with third countries see particularly a presentation as well as guidelines and concerns in EDPS, 'Opinion 2/2018 on eight negotiating mandates to conclude international agreements allowing the exchange of data between Europol and third countries' (14 March 2018) <https://edps.europa.eu/sites/edp/files/publication/18-03-19_opinion_international_agreements_europol_en.pdf> accessed on 3 February 2020.

of this divergence, and acknowledging that this is another field in which the requirements of human rights and respect for individual liberties have led to the conclusion that '*internal monitoring is inadequate given the extent of police powers and the particularly damaging consequences*', the Council's resolution calls for public prosecutors to 'scrutinise the lawfulness of police investigations at the latest when deciding whether a prosecution should commence or continue'.[299] In a similar direction, there are proposals on promoting 'judicial branches' within national police forces and conferring investigating duties upon them with regard to specific criminal offences.[300] Such views, which emanate from the contemporary reinforcement of police agencies in Europe, are particularly relevant to Europol.

As mentioned above, in recent years there has been a change of direction in the context of judicial cooperation in criminal matters in the EU. There may still be a long way to go, but promoting effectiveness almost at any cost had been so potent (especially) in EU law and case-law, that setting it aside for the sake of fundamental rights (as commented upon under section 8), no matter how restricted so far, is a significant change of stance that must determine future developments. And given that there is a concurrent evolution in the field of substantive criminal law, where the principle of legality is beginning to be assessed, even conditionally, as of primary importance compared to EU law effectiveness in recent CJEU case-law (which has even been called 'a victory of the concept of justice itself'),[301] similar standards must on the one hand also cover judicial cooperation *that concerns information sharing* and on the other hand apply as a notion to *police cooperation* as well.

---

299 Recommendation 'The Role Of Public Prosecution In The Criminal Justice System' Rec(2000)19, adopted by the Committee of Ministers of the Council of Europe on 6 October 2000, para 21; see also Dalakouras, *Criminal Procedure Law* 172–175. Similarly, UN Guidelines 'Police Operations in United Nations Peacekeeping Operations and Special Political Missions' [2015], para 16.

300 Dalakouras in *Criminal Procedure Law* 175 and in 'Concentrating evidence' [in Greek] [2011] Poinika Chronika 247, 254ff.

301 See the comment in Kaiafa-Gbandi, 'Supranational delineation of criminal repression' 504f, referring to Case C-42/17 *M.A.S. and M.B.* EU:C:2017:936 (see para 62); on that case see also Marco Bassini and Oreste Pollicino, 'Defusing the Taricco Bomb through Fostering Constitutional Tolerance: All Roads Lead to Rome' in <https://verfassungsblog.de/defusing-the-taricco-bomb-through-fostering-constitutional-tolerance-all-roads-lead-to-rome/> (accessed 3 February 2020); Dana Burchardt, 'Belittling the Primacy of EU Law in Taricco II' in <https://verfassungsblog.de/belittling-the-primacy-of-eu-law-in-taricco-ii/> (accessed 3 February 2020); Athina Giannakoula, 'Commentary on the Decision of the European Court of Justice of 5th December 2017' [in Greek] [2018] Revue Hellénique de Droit Européen, 84.

9.3 Principles Drawn from to the Rights of the Suspect/Accused

When it comes to the rights of the suspect or accused, an initial examination of fundamental rights leads us to identify the right to be presumed innocent and the privilege against self-incrimination as two rights which could in some way be transposed to the *precognitive* stage that we explore here. These rights can also be singled out since they are linked to a fundamental value choice that contemporary criminal law across the European area is connected to, namely the fact that we do not live in a suspect society where every citizen is constantly under surveillance. To the contrary, in order for criminal justice to be allowed to intrude into the affairs of a private individual, strict requirements must be adhered to. This is self-evident in the context of the presumption of innocence, which dictates that everyone is innocent until proven otherwise. Yet it is also philosophically connected to the privilege against self-incrimination, in the sense that there are limits to the lengths that state power can go to in order to satisfy its claim for criminal justice to be served, for instance by prohibiting the use of an individual as a means of evidence against themselves when it comes to self-incriminating statements. This underlying philosophical foundation of limiting state power with regard to investigating and punishing crimes is shared among these two rights, albeit in different forms and to a varying degree, and allows for an easier transposition into this *precognitive* stage, as it can be invoked to support the approach that they should be either applied or reflected in further requirements that must be established at this stage, as is argued below. Finally, even under US law, a jurisdiction that is considered one of the leading proponents in endorsing limitations of rights in order to combat terrorism, these rights still retain their distinct and uncontested value.[302]

302 The US has thus been chosen as a jurisdiction to examine and draw selected remarks from in order to flesh out the content of these two rights, to the extent that this is feasible and useful under the scope of this paper, not only because it is an important and leading jurisdiction in combatting terrorism globally as well as within the common law tradition, but also precisely due to its readiness to impose limitations on rights, as opposed to continental European law, which appears much more hesitant. See as an example of this difference in approach Stefan Sottiaux, *Terrorism and the Limitation of Rights-The ECHR and the US Constitution* (Hart Publishing 2008) 400–403, who points out the following: 'Although Article 6 [of the ECHR] is not listed among the non-derogable rights of Article 15, the European Convention practice contains no instances of derogations from one or more of the fair trial guarantees designed to deal with the problem of terrorism. (…) Despite the flexibility inherent in many of the Article 6 concepts, the creation of a special military judicial forum for terrorist offences would be so drastic a departure from the ordinary fair trial protections that it would fall below the minimum standards as set out in Article 6. Moreover, it is to be expected that, given the fundamental nature of most due process rights, the Strasbourg Court will take an active stance if called upon to review the strict necessity of derogating measures in this area, requiring for instance, detailed and

9.3.1 *The Right to Be Presumed Innocent*

The right to be presumed innocent is a fundamental right in the context of criminal proceedings and dates back to the origins of pivotal charters of rights such as the 'Declaration of the Rights of Man and of the Citizen' after the French Revolution or the Universal Declaration of Human Rights adopted by the UN.[303] It is now enshrined in milestone international human rights documents such as the International Covenant on Civil and Political Rights (ICCPR),[304] the American Convention on Human Rights (ACHR)[305] and the European Convention on Human Rights (ECHR).[306] In the context of the EU in particular, the presumption of innocence is prescribed under the Charter,[307] while it has also been the specific object of Directive (EU) 2016/343,[308] which states that its scope covers 'suspects or accused persons in criminal proceedings'.[309] The presumption of innocence is also enshrined in the domestic law of various countries.[310]

---

safeguards against abuse. (...) Notwithstanding the absence of an express constitutional basis for war and emergency restrictions on fundamental rights, the United States government established separate courts, operating special rules of procedures and evidence that differ from those applicable in the civilian legal system, to try certain categories of terrorist suspects.' See also for examples of legal experts and organisations raising concerns to limitations on the right to freedom of expression in the context of counter-terrorism legislation in Europe: Council of Europe, Commissioner for Human Rights, Human Rights Comment, 'Misuse of anti-terror legislation threatens freedom of expression', 4.12.2018 <www.coe.int/en/web/commissioner/-/misuse-of-anti-terror-legislation-threatens-freedom-of-expression>, accessed on 3 February 2020.

303 Stefan Trechsel, *Human Rights in Criminal Proceedings*, Chapter 7, 153–154.

304 Art 14(2).

305 Art 8(2).

306 Art 6(2).

307 Art 48(1).

308 Directive (EU) 2016/343 of 9 March 2016 on the strengthening of certain aspects of the presumption of innocence and of the right to be present at the trial in criminal proceedings [2016] OJ L 65/1.

309 Arts 2, 3, and 6.

310 Including Greece, see eg Androulakis, *Fundamental Principles* 217ff; Karras 28ff; Dalakouras, *Criminal Procedure Law* 106ff; Papadamakis, *Criminal Procedure* 14. Under US law in particular, the presumption of innocence plays a crucial role and it is said to 'undergird the American criminal justice system', while it is closely linked to the concept of due process and a fair trial. See on this point Shima Baradaran, 'The presumption of punishment' [2014] Crim Law and Philos 391, 391–392. The evolution of the presumption of innocence under US criminal law can be revealed by a shift in rules on bail that took place during the 1960s and the 1980s. Under US law due process guarantees the presumption of innocence and trial by jury, which initially resulted in a presumption of bail for every defendant—except on capital punishment trials—as only the jury at trial was permitted to make inferences on a defendant's guilt. Yet in the 1960s and 1980s federal laws

In Greece in particular, the presumption of innocence is recognised as a fundamental principle of the criminal trial and is considered as a necessary result of the principle of respect for human dignity.[311] It is enshrined under the ECHR and ICCPR, which form part of the Greek legal order,[312] and its reach extends to various stages of the criminal proceedings.[313] Under the recent amendment of the Code of Criminal Procedure by law 4620/2019, the presumption of innocence was expressly included. It is currently enshrined under article 71 of the new Code of Criminal Procedure, which states that 'Suspects and defendants are presumed innocent until their guilt is proven according to the law'.

The core of the right remains intact across the above legal documents and jurisdictions, as the presumption of innocence is primarily framed as a right awarded to persons who are being charged with an offence and has many aspects.[314] The practical implications of the presumption of innocence can be summarised as two main elements. First, in the context of the adversarial system, where the defendant and the prosecution are considered as the two opposing sides, it encompasses a *burden of proof* that rests on the prosecution, which means that, as a rule, no one can be subjected to criminal punishment unless the State (through the prosecution under the adversarial system) has established that they are guilty. Under the inquisitorial system, where the purpose of criminal trial and of the prosecution's role is to establish the truth, there is no such 'burden of proof' strictly speaking, as both sides seek to 'discover' the truth and not 'prove' guilt per se.[315] However, here again a burden of 'establishing' the truth can be identified, which rests on the judge. In other words, if through the fact-finding process of the criminal trial under the inquisitorial

---

were passed that gradually allowed for judges to weigh evidence against the defendant even at a pre-trial stage in order to make a determination on whether to grant or deny bail to a defendant. See Baradaran 401. This evolution shows that even in jurisdictions, like the US, where the presumption of innocence is deemed pivotal, its meaning can slightly shift over time. Husak also argues that the presumption of innocence has been 'eviscerated' under US criminal law; Douglas Husak, 'Social Engineering as an Infringement of the Presumption of Innocence: The Case of Corporate Criminality' [2014] Crim Law and Philos 353. For exceptions under English law, see also Victor Tadros, 'The Ideal of the Presumption of Innocence' [2014] Crim Law and Philos 449, 450.

311 Karras 28.

312 Androulakis, *Fundamental Principles* 222; Karras 28.

313 Androulakis, *Fundamental Principles* 221–222; Karras 29.

314 Karras 29. Stumer goes as far as to suggest that the presumption establishes that the 'state must not take coercive action against any individual unless it has been proved that the person is guilty of a criminal offence and is properly subject to punishment'; Andrew Stumer, *The Presumption of Innocence: Evidential and Human Rights Perspectives* (Hart Publishing 2010) xl.

315 Androulakis, *Fundamental Principles* 225–226.

system it is not established during the court hearing that the defendant is guilty, then they are to be found innocent, without it being necessary to fully establish their innocence instead. Secondly, it encompasses a *standard of proof*, which evolves throughout the criminal pre-trial and trial process, as will be outlined below, to culminate in the 'beyond reasonable doubt' requirement of guilt at the stage of sentencing in a criminal trial.[316]

The right to be presumed innocent can be invoked when criminal proceedings have been initiated,[317] with most international human rights documents using the wording 'charged' or 'accused' to describe who can benefit from the right. However, this presumption can also function before anyone is charged with a crime. This is readily confirmed by the fact that some legal instruments, such as Directive (EU) 2016/343, have extended their scope to cover suspects as well. Yet, on a more general note it is also proven based on two distinct arguments.

The first relates to the standard of proof referred to above, or what can also be described as the 'appropriate degree of suspicion' that follows each stage of the criminal proceedings.[318] This means that as we move from one stage to the next, the function of the presumption and the protection thereby awarded becomes more rigorous, in close connection to the increased infringement on an individual's rights that every next stage entails. A lesser degree of suspicion is needed in order to bring an individual in for questioning, a higher degree to charge him or her with a crime, an even higher degree to move the case to trial, and so on and so forth. This culminates in the criminal trial, the end stage of the proceedings, where the presumption of innocence manifests itself in such firm forms as the principle of *in dubio pro reo*, and the rule that the burden of proof is on the prosecuting authorities under the adversarial system or the burden of establishing guilt is on the judicial authorities under the inquisitorial system.

As such, in the same way that it is prohibited to convict someone while there are still doubts, it is also prohibited to move on to the next stage of the criminal proceedings or take judicial measures, which will damage the suspect's reputation and intrude on his or her personal life and liberties, without an increasingly elevated degree of suspicion.[319] In other words, there is an escalation to the

316 For these elements, see Husak, 'Social Engineering' 355.

317 See Thomas Weigend, 'Assuming that the Defendant Is Not Guilty: The Presumption of Innocence in the German System of Criminal Justice' [2014] Crim Law and Philos 285, 287.

318 This is a distinct principle under Greek criminal procedural law. See Karras 30; Theocharis Dalakouras, 'The principle of the appropriate degree of suspicion or power of indications' [in Greek] [2003] Poinikos Logos 1793.

319 Karras 30; Androulakis, *Fundamental Principles* 217.

intensity of the presumption according to the repercussions that each stage of the criminal stage entails, but its function starts already at the earlier pre-trial stages of investigating potential suspects or simply investigating a crime. This principle of the 'appropriate degree of suspicion'—also known as 'evidentiary standards' or 'standards of proof'—is widely recognised in national criminal law,[320] including Germany[321] and Greece.[322] Under US law, it is described by such evidentiary standards such as—in order of intensity—'reasonable suspicion', 'probable cause', 'beyond the shadow of a doubt' etc.[323]

This evolving intensity points to the fact that it is not the pressing of criminal charges that first gives rise to the presumption of innocence. To the contrary, it often spills over to the preventive activities of law enforcement authorities, when there is still no specific criminal charge. In this context, it functions as a limitation to the powers of law enforcement authorities to subject individuals to surveillance and other measures such as searching a person or their possessions or property. Very often, searching or investigating someone is only permitted when there is at least a suspicion that they are connected to a criminal act.[324] In order to safeguard the soundness of judgment with regard to the existence of such suspicions, criminal procedure law as a rule mandates that a judicial ruling must be procured in order to legitimise the actions of law enforcement authorities, e.g. that a search warrant must be issued in order to search a property, or that electronic surveillance is allowed *in concreto* by virtue of an order issued by the prosecutor, etc.

This is further evident also in the context of information systems examined under this paper: for example, in the case of SIS II it is expressly stated that alerts for the purpose of *discreet or specific checks*, which are *preventive* in nature, are only permitted when there is 'clear indication' that a person intends to commit or is committing a serious criminal offence, or where an 'overall assessment' of a person gives reason to suspect they will commit such crimes.[325]

320 Kai Ambos, *Treatise on International Criminal Law: Volume III: International Criminal Procedure* (OUP 2016) 397; Erwin Chemerinsky and Laurie Levenson, *Criminal Procedure: Investigation* (3rd edn, Wolters Kluwer 2018) 420ff.

321 Björn Elberling, *The Defendant in International Criminal Proceedings* (Hart Publishing 2012) 151ff.

322 Karras 30; Androulakis, *Fundamental Principles* 217.

323 See the *Terry standard* as formulated by the US Supreme Court in *Terry v. Ohio*, 392 U.S. 1 (1968).

324 See also above, section 9.2. This is safeguarded also by the right to liberty as well as the right to respect someone's private and family life, home and communications. See Charter arts 6 and 7; ECHR arts 5 and 8.

325 See above, section 2.1.1.

The second argument relates to the reasoning behind the presumption of innocence. While it is clearly delineated in relevant human rights documents as applying when a person is *charged* with an offence, it would be absurd to claim that everyone who is *not charged* with an offence is somehow presumed guilty or could be subject to law enforcement actions without any further prerequisites. Instead, in societies where law is based on the principles of democracy, personal liberty, and freedom of thought and expression, anything that is not expressly forbidden is prima facie allowed, hence criminal justice must have a specific legal and factual basis in order to meddle in the affairs of private individuals.

Instead, the wording used in such human rights documents can be explained if we consider the following: it is precisely when someone is *charged* with an offence that the shadow of suspicion is already placed upon him or her. This is why those drafting the provisions safeguarding the presumption of innocence felt the need to specify that the presumption *still holds* even when someone is charged with a crime, rather than that this is the first instance when the presumption begins to function. In other words, a person is *still presumed* innocent *even though we now have suspicions against them*. A fortiori, everyone who has not yet been charged with a crime benefits from the presumption.[326] The difference is that we seldom encounter a reason to invoke the presumption of innocence unless an individual is somehow caught in the web of criminal justice.

However, in the scope of this paper, we could identify such an instance. It could be argued that, to the extent that in the context of the information systems examined in this paper, we can identify a 'hidden' *precognitive* function of law enforcement authorities that primarily takes place at an earlier stage by the mass collection of *potentially relevant* data on persons that could be unrelated to crimes, a new rule should be established based on the presumption of innocence and its aspect of requiring an appropriate degree of *suspicion* that should regulate the conduct and powers of law enforcement authorities when their agents carry out checks and searches with regard to individuals.

This rule should mandate that, even at this *precognitive* stage, an adequate degree of suspicion that corresponds to the law enforcement activity taking place should be introduced that would serve as the measure by which the relevant legislative acts would provide for a narrower or broader degree of

326 See also Trechsel 155–156, with slightly different argumentation, as well as Hamish Stewart, 'The right to be presumed innocent' [2014] Crim Law and Philos 407, 409, who argues that the presumption of innocence also applies before trial, linking it to what he calls 'the right to be without reproach'.

investigative powers. It is important to note that it might sometimes be the case that, under this new criminal law paradigm described above, law enforcement authorities might need to first have access to personal data before they can identify a pattern or other indicators that will give rise to such a suspicion. As such, it is not practical to suggest that blanket personal data processing, such as in the case of PNR, should never take place, but rather turn our attention towards delineating the safeguards and limitations that should be imposed on this law enforcement activity.

In order to examine these limitations, we can identify a spectrum of cases that would justify law enforcement involvement, depending on two main elements:

a. the probability of a *criminal act* having been committed or being currently underway or being in the process of potentially taking place in the future, and
b. the potential involvement of a specific *individual*, whose data is being collected and processed.

As such, at the one end of the spectrum we can identify the case where regarding element (a) no crime has been committed nor do law enforcement authorities have any indication that a crime will be committed, and regarding (b) there is no indication that a specific individual is connected to any crime. On the other end of the spectrum, there is the case of, regarding (a) a crime having been committed or being in the process of being committed (either at the attempt stage or closely before that, at the stage of criminalised preparatory acts), and regarding (b) law enforcement authorities having connected this criminal activity to a specific individual. In between these two extremes, there is a wide range of cases, for example when a crime has been committed but law enforcement authorities have no indication as to which individuals are possibly connected to the crime, or when law enforcement authorities have connected a specific individual to criminal activity (e.g. suspected terrorist activity) but they have not yet connected them with a specific crime.

In the case of the first end of the spectrum, there is hardly any suspicion that a criminal act took or will take place, nor any suspicion that any individual could be involved. In that case, the collection of personal data, or the use of personal data already collected for other non-law enforcement purposes, should be carried out with the highest level of caution. On the contrary, in the case of the other end of the spectrum, it is obvious that gathering and processing some types of personal data could play a crucial role for law enforcement authorities trying to prevent or investigate a crime. As we move from one extreme of the spectrum to the other, and in line with the rule of an 'appropriate degree of suspicion' and the principle of proportionality, the way that data is collected should differentiate. These nuances should have an impact on what types of data are collected, relating to which individuals, how they could be used or shared, for how long they could be retained, etc.

As such, the following structure could be formulated, where law enforcement data processing operates on three distinct data pool levels:

i. the *scope* of data collection and processing—ranging from mass collection from every data subject (e.g. every passenger on a plane), to only collecting specific information from a specific individual,
ii. the *types* of data collected—ranging from data that is connected to criminal acts in an obvious manner, to a series of seemingly 'innocent' data that appears unrelated to criminal activities, and
iii. the *intensity of the link with a criminal act*—ranging from data being sought in connection to a specific crime, to collecting data even when there is no indication of criminal activity.

As the degree of suspicion gets higher, appropriate action should be taken gradually on each level. For instance, at the early stages when there is a low degree of suspicion, data may readily be collected (i) from a *specific* passenger, (ii) when this data is *connected* to a potential criminal activity or could help further elucidate it, and (iii) when *there are suspicions* that criminal activity which falls under the scope of the information systems examined therein (i.e. terrorism and serious crime) will probably take place and that the specific individual under (i) is involved in it.

As we move towards stronger suspicions, we could conceive of these elements as 'communicating vessels' of sorts, where very strong and precise suspicions on one level could excuse a much lesser degree of suspicion on another. For example, if there are strong suspicions or certainty that a specific individual is connected to a crime, even when the specifics of the crime are still vague, then we could see the point in allowing a wider pool of data to be gathered from this individual and we could even understand that it could be useful to extend that collection to other individuals connected to him or her, e.g. persons traveling together. On the other hand, when there is clear intelligence that a crime will be committed, but we do not have any indication as to who exactly from a pool of data subjects is connected to it, we could again see the point in allowing data connected to that crime to be gathered from every data subject in that pool, even from people who will later be proven to have nothing to do with this crime.

As such, even though we cannot completely rule out the possibility of blanket collection of personal data, even when there is no indication of a crime, we could argue in favour of restricting the scope of law enforcement activity and the types of personal data collected in such a case. Data retention periods are also pivotal as a limitation in this respect, as they could allow us to differentiate across this spectrum of the appropriate degree of suspicion on each level. Thus, even when there is mass collection (i) of various types of data (ii), e.g. in the case of PNR data described above, then these should only be retained for a short period of time within which law enforcement authorities will have had the chance to scour them for clues or link them to criminal activity (iii). After that shorter retention period, any data identified as connected to a criminal act could be retained for longer, but any data not thus connected should be permanently deleted.

9.3.2 *The Privilege against Self-Incrimination*

The right not to incriminate oneself is a fundamental right in the context of criminal proceedings. It is explicitly enshrined in international human rights documents such as the ICCPR,[327] and the ACHR.[328] Although the ECHR contains no such explicit reference, it is widely accepted that the right not to incriminate oneself is implicit in the right to a fair trial under article 6(1) of the Convention, as has been recognised in the case-law of the ECtHR from 1993 onwards.[329] A similar approach is taken in the context of article 48 of the Charter, which safeguards the 'rights of the defence' for anyone charged.[330] Yet the principle against self-incrimination as well as the right to silence are explicitly included in the aforementioned Directive (EU) 2016/343.[331]

The origins of the right trace back to religious law and its evolution is closely connected to common law.[332] Under US law, the privilege against

327 Art 14(3).

328 Art 8(2),(3).

329 Trechsel 361. Council of Europe, *Guide on Article 6 of the European Convention on Human Rights—Right to a fair trial (criminal limb)*, updated on 31 December 2019 <www.echr.coe.int/Documents/Guide_Art_6_criminal_ENG.pdf> accessed 3 February 2020. Theodoros Papakyriakou, *The principle of non self-incrimination in light of the recent case-law of the ECHR* (Nomiki Bibliothiki 2009) 1ff. ECtHR, *John Murray v the UK* (Application no. 18731/91), Judgment, 8 February 1996, para 45.

330 Hanns Peter Nehl, 'Article 48(1)—Presumption of Innocence' in Steve Peers and others, *The EU Charter of Fundamental Rights: A Commentary* (Hart Publishing 2014) 1278.

331 See art 7 of the Directive. See also art 2 for its temporal scope, where it is stated that the privilege relates to persons suspected or accused in the context of criminal proceedings.

332 Trechsel 341; Papakyriakou 3; Olga Tsolka, 'The right to non self-incrimination and the presumption of innocence' [in Greek] [2004] Poinika Chronika 97. Tsolka in particular traces the origins of the right back to Talmudic law—see Olga Tsolka, *The 'nemo tenetur se ipsum prodere/accusare' principle in the criminal trial* [in Greek] (PN Sakkoulas 2002) 7–10. But also Richard Helmholz, 'Origins of the Privilege against Self-Incrimination: The Role of the European Ius Commune' [1990] New York University Law Review 962.

self-incrimination is also considered as pivotal for the functioning of the criminal justice system and forms part of the US Constitution.[333] Under continental European law, that is, across civil law jurisdictions, the privilege against self-incrimination holds a central place under national criminal procedure law.[334] In German law in particular, which is considered a civil law jurisdiction of substantial influence when it comes to criminal law, the privilege was first recognised in the mid-19th century.[335] Up until then, the individual was subjected to the inquisitorial system and was handled as an evidentiary means to establish the truth.[336]

In Greece, the sources of the privilege against self-incrimination are found in the ICCPR and the ECHR.[337] Just like with the presumption of innocence, the privilege against self-incrimination was also expressly included in the new Greek Code or Criminal Procedure, by virtue of its recent amendment under law 4620/2019. It is currently enshrined under article 104(1) of the new Code of Criminal Procedure, which states that 'the suspect or the accused has the

333 The powerful impact of the privilege against self-incrimination under American criminal law has led scholars to declare its appearance as a 'landmark event in Anglo-American criminal procedure'. It is important to note in this respect that under US law, the privilege against self-incrimination forms part of the US Constitution, as it is enshrined under the Fifth Amendment that passed into law in 1791, which states among others that no person 'shall be compelled in any criminal case to be a witness against himself'. See the Fifth Amendment text under the Cornell University archives, at <www.law.cornell.edu/constitution/fifth_amendment> accessed 3 February 2020. As it has evolved across time, according to the account given by John Langbein, the privilege against self-incrimination has undergone a profound shift from the initial privilege not to accuse oneself to the contemporary rendition that an accused has the right to not to respond or testify. According to Langbein's comparative account, the privilege against self-incrimination has across jurisdictions evolved to encompass the right not to be subjected to torture to the modern US prohibition of drawing a negative inference due to the accused's silence; John Langbein, 'The historical origins of the privilege against self-incrimination at common law' [1994] Michigan Law Review, 1047, 1084–1085.

334 See for instance §136 of the German STOP (Strafprozessordnung) <www.gesetze-im-internet.de/stpo/__136.html> accessed 3 February 2020, art 520.2 of the Spanish Ley de Enjuiciamiento Criminal <http://noticias.juridicas.com/base_datos/Penal/lecr.l2t6.html> accessed 3 February 2020, article 116 of the French Code de procédure pénale <www.legislationline.org/documents/section/criminal-codes/country/30/France/show> accessed 3 February 2020, art 103A of the Greek Code of Criminal Procedure. For Greece, see in particular Adam Papadamakis, *Applications of Criminal Procedure* [in Greek] (Nomiki Vivltiothiki 2006) 36–40.

335 Tsolka, *Nemo tenetur* 37ff, with further references. On the content of the privilege in practice, see, inter alia, BVerfGE 56, 37; NJW 1981, 1431 and BVerfG, 07.07.1995-2 BvR 326/92, StV 1995, 505.

336 Tsolka, *Nemo tenetur* 37ff.

337 Papakyriakou 1–2.

right to silence and to non-self-incrimination'. Under article 104(2) of the Code of Criminal Procedure, it is also provided that the privilege against self-incrimination shall not impede the lawful gathering of evidence that exists irrespective of the will of the suspect or the accused, while under Article 104(3) it is expressly stated that no negative inferences may be drawn against the suspect or accused due to the exercise of the right to silence and to non-self-incrimination. The privilege against self-incrimination is also referred to under article 95 of the new Code of Criminal Procedure, as one of the rights that the suspect or the accused has the right to be informed of.

In practice, under Greek law the privilege against self-incrimination is conceived as a liberal procedural principle that safeguards the rights of the accused by limiting the ways in which evidence may be lawfully gathered and used in the context of criminal proceedings.[338] Its content can be summarised in four distinct elements, as the prohibition of (a) *compelling* someone (b) to make *self-incriminating statements* (c) when they are *charged* (d) with a *specific offence*.[339]

The privilege has also been firmly affirmed in the ECtHR case law in the context of the ECHR, as has been noted above, which is a testament to the fact that it forms part of a broader European legal culture with regard to criminal procedure rights. Finally, the CJEU has also affirmed the existence of the privilege in the context of competition law cases, where administrative sanctions may be imposed which reflect a punitive element, but also where useful information can be extracted in order to be used later in criminal proceedings.[340]

Although the exact content of the right is not universally agreed upon,[341] its core can be summarised as the right not to be compelled to provide information that might contribute to incriminating oneself with regard to the commission of a crime. In that sense, the right is closely connected to the right to silence—and by extension, the right of the defendant not to have negative inferences drawn against them if they choose to remain silent—while it also serves to protect the defendant against facing charges of perjury, obstruction of justice, etc. when it is discovered that they have lied or withheld crucial information in order not to incriminate themselves.

The right not to incriminate oneself mainly pertains to testimonial evidence, that is, evidence 'created' on the spot by the accused or suspect when answering questions or orders of the investigating authorities. This means that

338 Papakyriakou 4.

339 As summarised by Papakyriakou 4.

340 See Case C-374/87 *Orkem v Commission* EU:C:1989:387 and Case 27/88 *Solvay & Cie v Commission of the European Communities* EU:C:1989:388.

341 Tsolka, *Nemo tenetur* 15ff; Papakyriakou 3ff.

a suspect or accused may be obliged to allow the discovery of evidence that will incriminate them, e.g. by being subjected to a search of their house, their car, their bags etc. even against their will. As such, both the ECtHR[342] and the US Supreme Court[343] have found that, while the right does not absolve anyone from being obliged to hand over *documents* required by the investigating authorities, being compelled to produce documents which the investigating authorities cannot adequately describe or are unsure whether they exist infringes on the right not to incriminate oneself. Under US law, this distinction is known as the 'act-of-production doctrine' and relies on the argument that by producing such documents the defendant would be essentially testifying with regard to the existence, possession, chain of custody and/or authenticity of such documents, which is prohibited when this would be incriminating in and of itself.

As such, it is evident that an overview of the right reveals that its scope is prima facie narrow, in contrast to what has been said above with regard to the presumption of innocence. The right not to incriminate oneself may be invoked *after* criminal proceedings have been initiated, extending to the pre-trial stage and any functionally equivalent proceedings.[344] However, it does not extend beyond that, as it clashes with the powers of police and other law enforcement authorities to prevent and investigate crimes. As such, there is a wide spectrum of permitted law enforcement activities, where an individual's self-incriminatory remarks or acts may be taken into account, ranging from undercover police activity to electronic surveillance.

However, there are three important conditions in order for this undisclosed police activity to take place lawfully. The first relates to the 'compelled' element of the rule. The self-incriminating remarks or acts, which may be permissibly recorded and used, must be carried out based on the individual's free will and should not be the result of coercion or incitement. This is why entrapment and the actions of agents provocateurs are generally prohibited.[345]

---

342 ECtHR, Funke v. France, Judgment, 25 February 1993, § 44.

343 United States v. Hubbell, 530 U.S. 27 (2000), examining the right not to incriminate oneself under the Fifth Amendment.

344 See eg Tsolka, *Nemo tenetur* 157–161.

345 See ECtHR, Khudobin v. Russia, para 128; Matanović v. Croatia, para 122; Ramanauskas v. Lithuania (no. 2), paras 51–55. Also Alexandros Dimakis, 'Recent developments in ECtHR case-law on police entrapment and the impact on Greek case-law' [in Greek] [2008] Poinika Chronika 594; Adam Papadamakis, 'Police entrapment: Limitations and transgressions' [in Greek] [2010] Poiniki Dikaiosyni 1326, 1327–1328; and Maria Kaiafa-Gbandi, 'The recent case-law of ECtHR on police entrapment and the right to a fair trial' [in Greek] [2011] Poiniki Dikaiosyni 59, 65–67, who points out that, under the ECtHR case law, agents provocateurs are required to assume only an 'essentially passive role'. See also Papadamakis, *Applications of Criminal Procedure* 85ff and in particular 89–90.

The second condition is that whenever such a law enforcement activity takes place, it is in the context of an investigation into criminal activity. Although it may be the case that no potential crimes have been specifically identified, and the law enforcement activity aims precisely at uncovering or identifying them, there is at the very least a strong indication that allowing such surveillance could help prevent or detect crimes.

This is related to the third condition: that such an undercover law enforcement activity must as a rule be authorised or supervised by a judicial authority, which often permits the surveillance activity to take place and subjects it to further limitations, including temporal limits, its scope, limits with regard to which persons should be investigated, etc. This is connected to the function of the police and similar law enforcement agencies to prevent, detect and investigate crimes (in some cases other public authorities like the fire service also take on some investigative duties), but not necessarily to the broader role of law enforcement in safeguarding public safety and public order.

When these three conditions are not met, e.g. when a police agent incites a perpetrator, or when he or she carries out surveillance without a warrant to do so, or when such a warrant is unlawfully issued absent any indication that there is potential criminal activity, then this surveillance activity should be deemed unlawful.

In this context, it could be argued that when data is gathered and processed in the context of the *precognitive* function outlined above (in section 9.1), then these philosophical foundations underlying the prohibition of self-incrimination should give rise to specific safeguards. First of all, it should be taken into account that the data subjects are *compelled* in the context of the information systems examined by this paper to provide the requested data. This should be taken into consideration already at the stage of deciding *which* types of data may be collected. It is therefore important to draw analogies with regard to data that could amount to such testimonial incriminating evidence, as being compelled to provide such information would be prohibited by the right not to incriminate oneself. Even though as EU information systems have been set up in present it cannot be argued that data subjects are compelled to provide types of data that resemble testimonial evidence, and which would *directly* incriminate them, this limitation should be taken into account when updating these systems (e.g. by expanding them to collect new types of data) or when establishing new information systems.

Furthermore, since they are *compelled* to do so, data subjects should only be asked to provide *potentially or indirectly* incriminating data *after* being informed of how this data may be used for the purposes of combating crime and in the context of criminal proceedings, so that they can decide in an informed manner whether or not they wish to share this information. It is important to note that even data which prima facie seems 'innocent' could be potentially or indirectly incriminating data. For instance, information collected on airplane baggage could reveal which passengers are potentially legally travelling with firearms, which could be then linked to criminal activity, while passenger seat data could be used to connect seemingly unrelated passengers with each other, which is particularly useful when one of them is under surveillance due to suspicions of involvement with terrorist activity. A proper and informed choice on part of the passenger whose data would be collected could be encouraged, for example in the case of PNR data, by displaying a relevant information message at the time of check-in. This could be similar to messages which inform passengers about which items they are not allowed to carry with them on the plane, in order to ensure that they have at least the opportunity to have access to that information at the time of booking or check-in.

As the situation stands at present, even though fundamental information about how the EU information systems examined herein may be used for combating crime is accessible to anyone, as the relevant legislative documents are publicly disclosed, it can hardly be argued that individuals are aware of these potential uses when they hand over their data. This is evident when we take into account that the architecture of the information systems is complex, the relevant documents large in volume and loaded with specialist terminology, meaning that special legal or even IT expertise is often required to understand them, and how they are applied in practice remains largely obscure to the wider public. This is, after all, part of the purpose that this paper aims to serve—to shed more light to how data in the EU information systems may be collected and processed for the purpose of combating crime.

Lastly, it would be important to include institutional safeguards to this *precognitive* activity of law enforcement, equivalent to the rule that usual law enforcement surveillance activity should be monitored and accordingly allowed or prohibited by a superior, impartial and independent judicial authority on a case-by-case basis. Such a process could refer to the relevant internal procedures of each Member State, or, as the EU moves towards broader unification, this could be an opportunity for institutions such as the European Data Protection Supervisor, subject to a respective revision of its mandate, or a potential future European Criminal Court,[346] to play a safeguarding role.

346 See Kaiafa-Gbandi, 'CJEU case law and the European Arrest Warrant (Part B)' 153.

Conclusions

The above analysis leads us to some useful conclusions with regard to the role of information systems in the EU and more generally with regard to a new paradigm of criminal law. First of all, it is evident that the information systems established under EU law form a significant part of EU policy with regard to law enforcement. In this context, it is important to note the fact that the legislative landscape of the EU information systems is particularly complicated and difficult to follow, with various legal tools governing the operation of a single system, partial amendments and extensions introduced by later legislative documents, several proposals undergoing a series of updates, and finally long periods between legal tools getting voted and getting published or coming into effect. This picture is particularly worrying when we take into consideration that these information systems play a pivotal role in the field of security and criminal law, so it is important for both EU and third country citizens to be able to have easy and effective access to this legislative landscape and understand its scope and its limits.

Secondly, it must be noted in this same context that many of the information systems examined under this paper were first or primarily established with a purpose that did not relate directly to criminal law, e.g. for the management of borders, but their mandate was extended in order to provide access rights to law enforcement authorities and Europol. This further complicates the point illustrated above with regard to the fact that it is not easy for citizens to follow what each information system covers and how the data collected could be put to use. Yet it also raises another concern, since, when these systems were set up, they were designed with a specific scope and objectives in mind, which did not include law enforcement gaining access to the data gathered and processed, or included it as a secondary aim. Thus, the possibility always remains that when a system is being designed with the purpose of serving two very different aims, one of them being the aim of serving security and streamlining law enforcement activity, and especially when the latter was later added, then its architecture, scope, safeguards, etc. need to be envisioned and implemented taking both aims into account. Especially when a system is later extended to cover law enforcement purposes, then this should function in two different directions: both in designing the systems in a way that would be more effective for law enforcement, and in introducing further institutional and architectural safeguards against abuse of power. In any case, if it is the intention of the EU legislator to serve law enforcement purposes as well, then this should be stated clearly and be openly and justifiably pursued; if such an aim affects the systems only indirectly, then it would very likely enable abuse.

Thirdly, it is important to point out that this complex landscape is once again further complicated by the introduction of interoperability. The new interoperability framework is set to bring together systems that function at different speeds: information systems already in use, as well as information systems that have been legislatively established but have not yet been implemented. Besides the obvious upheaval that will again enhance the obscurity and complexity of the EU information systems landscape, interoperability is also set to contribute to the culture of casual connection between law enforcement and the systems. Despite its declared aim of functioning within a limited scope and having a purely technical character, interoperability will in fact cause a paradigm shift when it comes to how these information systems function, will result in broader law enforcement access rights, and reinforce the underlying link between the EU information systems and the objective of serving security and criminal law aims. The objections that have been raised with regard to the new regime, including concerns raised by EU organs like the EDPS, attest to this respect.

Fourth, as this connection to criminal law and law enforcement purposes becomes all the more clear, and recent developments indicate that it will continue to be reinforced, it is important to place the EU information systems correctly within a broader emerging paradigm shift in criminal law. In this respect, it is important to note that criminal law at the EU level, and subsequently at the national law level across Member States that are called upon to transpose and implement EU legislation, is undergoing a fundamental transformation. By construing prima facie neutral acts as crimes, recent anti-terrorist legislation serves as the driving force behind this transformation, which sees criminal law encompass a *pre-preventive* stage within its scope. The central role awarded to information under this stage is, on the one side, progressively strengthening the role of the police and, on the other side, giving rise to what can be called the new emerging *precognitive* paradigm under criminal law. Under this emerging paradigm, mass collection of a wide pool of data is carried out, even when this data is not connected to any crime, with the aim of using, for law enforcement purposes, any data that is at a later stage found to be linked to criminal activity. This can be again understood in the wider context of a culture that enables casual access of law enforcement authorities to large volumes of personal data, as has been outlined above.

Finally, against this setting of a new *precognitive stage in criminal law*, where information is elevated to serve a pivotal role in the *anticipation* of criminal activity, and in light of the disturbing expansion of police powers in the EU, we must also search for limitations and safeguards that will counterbalance this extended law enforcement activity and uphold the liberal principles of contemporary criminal law. This is especially urgent since this new law enforcement field does not fall under the traditional stages of criminal law which are already regulated and subject to limitations. In order to not let this law enforcement activity go unchecked, we have to turn to fundamental principles and rights that govern later stages of the criminal justice process and examine whether they could in some way function already at this *precognitive* stage. In this context, limitations for *precognitive* law enforcement activity could be drawn from the principle of proportionality, as well as the presumption of innocence and the privilege against self-incrimination.

Bibliography

Alexiadis S., *Human Rights in Criminal Policy: twelve studies* [in Greek] (Sakkoulas 1990).

Alexiadis S., *Crime Investigation* [in Greek] (Sakkoulas 2006).

Allegrezza S., 'Collecting criminal evidence across the European Union: the European Investigation Order between flexibility and proportionality' in Ruggeri S. (ed), *Transnational evidence and multicultural inquiries in Europe* (Springer 2014) 51.

Ambos K., *Treatise on International Criminal Law: Volume III: International Criminal Procedure* (OUP 2016).

Anagnostopoulou D. (ed), *Developments and challenges of the EU area of freedom, security and justice: proceedings of the International Conference in the memory of Dimitrios Evrigenis* (University of Macedonia Press 2015) ch 1–3.

Androulakis N., 'The limits of the investigative action and the principle of proportionality' [in Greek] [1975] Poinika Chronika 3.

Androulakis N., *Fundamental Principles of Criminal Procedure Law* [in Greek] (4th, PN Sakkoulas 2012).

Ashworth A., *Principles of Criminal Law* (OUP 2006).

Asp P., 'Two Notions of Proportionality' in Nuotio K. and Lahti R. (eds), *Festschrift in honour of Raimo Lahti* (University of Helsinki 2007) 207.

Asp P., *The Procedural Criminal Law Cooperation of the EU* (Stockholm University 2016).

Bachmaier L., 'Towards the Transposition of Directive 2014/41 regarding the European Investigation Order in Criminal Matters' [2015] Eucrim 47.

Bachmaier L., 'Countering terrorism: Suspects without suspicion and (pre-)suspects under surveillance' in Sieber U. and others (eds), *Alternative Systems of Crime Control: National, Transnational, and International Dimensions* (Duncker & Humblot 2018) 171.

Baker E. and Harding C., From past imperfect to future perfect? A longitudinal study of the Third Pillar [2009] European Law Review 25.

Barack A., *Proportionality Constitutional Rights and their Limitations* (Cambridge University Press 2012) 129.

Baradaran S., 'The presumption of punishment' [2014] Crim Law and Philos 391.

Bargis M., 'Personal Freedom and Surrender' in Kostoris R.E. (ed), *Handbook on European criminal procedure* (Springer 2018) 297.

Bassini M. and Pollicino O., 'Defusing the Taricco Bomb through Fostering Constitutional Tolerance: All Roads Lead to Rome' in <https://verfassungsblog.de/defusing-the-taricco-bomb-through-fostering-constitutional-tolerance-all-roads-lead-to-rome/> (accessed 3 February 2020).

Belfiore R., 'European Investigation Order in Criminal Matters: Developments in Evidence gathering across Europe' [2015] European Criminal Law Review 316.

Biagioni G., 'Avotinš v. Latvia—The Uneasy Balance Between Mutual Recognition of Judgments and Protection of Fundamental Rights' [2016] European Papers 579.

Boehm F., *Information Sharing and Data Protection in the Area of Freedom, Security and Justice* (Spinger 2012).

Böse M., 'The Principle of Proportionality and the Protection of Legal Interests (Verhältnismäßigkeit und Rechtsgüterschutz)' [2011] European Criminal Law Review 35.

Bowers J., 'Punishing the innocent' [2008] University of Pennsylvania Law Review 1117.

Burchardt D., 'Belittling the Primacy of EU Law in Taricco II' in <https://verfassungsblog.de/belittling-the-primacy-of-eu-law-in-taricco-ii/> (accessed 3 February 2020).

Carrera S. and Mitsilegas V., *Upholding the Rule of Law by scrutinising judicial independence-The Irish Court's request for a preliminary ruling on the European Arrest Warrant* (CEPS 2018) (*Constitutionalising*).

Chemerinsky E. and Levenson L., *Criminal Procedure: Investigation* (3rd edn, Wolters Kluwer 2018).

Clifford D. and Ausloos J., 'Data Protection and the Role of Fairness' (CiTiP Working Paper 29/2017, August 3 2017) in <https://ssrn.com/abstract=3013139> accessed 3 February 2020).

Curtin D., 'Security of the Interstice and Interoperable Data Sharing: A First Cut' in Carrera S. and Mitsilegas V. (eds), *Constitutionalising the Security Union* (CEPS 2017) 65.

Dalakouras T., *The Principle of Proportionality and procedural coercive measures* [in Greek] (Sakkoulas 1993).

Dalakouras T., 'The principle of the appropriate degree of suspicion or power of indications' [in Greek] [2003] Poinikos Logos 1793.

Dalakouras T., 'The Principle of Proportionality and procedural coercive measures' [in Greek] [2005] Poinika Chronika 961.

Dalakouras T., 'Concentrating evidence' [in Greek] [2011] Poinika Chronika 247.

Dalakouras T., *Criminal Procedure Law—Volume 1* [in Greek] (PN Sakkoulas 2012).

Daniele M. and Calvanese E., 'Evidence Gathering' in Kostoris R.E. (ed), *Handbook on European criminal procedure* (Springer 2018) 353.

Daskalopoulos S., 'European Investigation Order (EIO): The new Institution of Judicial Cooperation in Criminal Matters in the European Union' [in Greek] [2018] Poinika Chronika 173.

De Amicis G., 'Horizontal Cooperation' in Kostoris R.E. (ed), *Handbook on European criminal procedure* (Springer 2018) 249.

De Amicis G. and Kostoris R.E., 'Vertical Cooperation' in Kostoris R.E. (ed), *Handbook on European criminal procedure* (Springer 2018) 201.

De Hert P. and Sajfert J., 'The role of Data Protection Authorities in supervising police and criminal justice authorities processing personal data' in Briere C. and Weyembergh A. (eds), *The Needed Balances in EU Criminal Law: Past, Present and Future* (Hart Publishing 2018) 243.

Dimakis A., 'Recent developments in ECtHR case-law on police entrapment and the impact on Greek case-law' [in Greek] [2008] Poinika Chronika 594.

Długosz J., 'The Principle of Proportionality in European Union Law as a Prerequisite for Penalization' [2017] Adam Mickiewicz University Law Review 283.

Docksey C., 'Opinion 1/15: Privacy and security, finding the balance' [2017] Maastricht Journal of European and Comparative Law 768.

Dubber M., 'Theories of Crime and Punishment in German Criminal Law' [2006] The American Journal of Comparative Law 679.

Duff R.A., 'Harms and Wrongs' (2001) Buffalo Criminal Law Review 13.

Duff R.A. and Marshall S., '"Remote Harms" and the Two Harm Principles' in Simester A.P., du Bois-Pedain A. and Neumann U. (eds), *Liberal Criminal Law Theory, Essays for Andreas von Hirsch* (Hart Publishing 2014) 205.

Eisele J., 'Datenverkehr und Datenschutz im Rahmen der polizeilichen und justiziellen Zusammenarbeit' in Max-Planck-Institut für ausländisches und internationales Strafrecht and others (eds), *Europäisches Strafrecht* (Nomos Verlag 2014) 877.

Eisele K., 'Interoperability between EU information systems for security, border and migration management' (*European Parliamentary Research Service* February 2018) PE 615.649.

Elberling B., *The Defendant in International Criminal Proceedings* (Hart Publishing 2012).

Eser A., 'The Principle of "Harm" in the Crime Concept: A Comparative Analysis of the Criminally Protected Legal Interests' [1996] 4 Duquesne University Law Review 345.

European Criminal Policy Initiative, 'A Manifesto on European Criminal Procedure' [2013] ZIS 430.

Feiler L., Forgó N. and Weigl M., *The EU General Data Protection Regulation (GDPR): A Commentary* (Globe Law & Business 2018).

Feinberg J., *The Moral Limits of the Criminal Law (Oxford: Oxford University Press): Harm to Others (1984); Offense to Others (1985); Harm to Self (1986); Harmless Wrongdoing (1988).*

Fiodorova A., *Information Exchange and EU Law Enforcement* (1st edn, Routledge 2018).

Garcimartín Montero R., 'The European Investigation Order and the Respect for Fundamental Rights in Criminal Investigations' [2017] Eucrim 45.

Garland D., 'The Limits of the Sovereign State: Strategies of Crime Control in Contemporary Society' [1996] British Journal of Criminology 445.

Giannakoula A., *Crime and Sanctions in the European Union* [in Greek] (Nomiki Bibliothiki 2015).

Giannakoula A., 'The European Agenda on Security—A Comment' [2016] European Criminal Law Review 99.

Giannakoula A., 'Commentary on the Decision of the European Court of Justice of 5th December 2017' [in Greek] [2018] Revue Hellénique de Droit Européen 84.

Gless S., 'Europol' in Mitsilegas V., Bergström M. and Konstadinides T. (eds), *Research Handbook on EU Criminal Law* (Elgar 2016) 457.

Guild E., *Merging Security from Two-Level Game: Inserting the Treaty of Prüm into EU law?* (CEPS 2007).

Guild E. and Geyer F., *Getting local: Schengen, Prüm and the dancing procession of Echternach; Three paces forward and two back for EU police and judicial cooperation* (CEPS 2006).

Gutiérrez Zarza Á., *Exchange of Information and Data Protection in Cross-border Criminal Proceedings in Europe* (Springer 2015).

Hassemer W., 'The Harm Principle and the Protection of 'Legal Goods' (Rechtsgüterschutz): a German Perspective' in Simester A.P., du Bois-Pedain A. and Neumann U. (eds), *Liberal Criminal Law Theory, Essays for Andreas von Hirsch* (Hart Publishing 2014) 187.

Hecker B., *Europäisches Strafrecht* (Springer 2015).

Hefendehl R., von Hirsch A. and Wohlers W., *Die Rechtsgutstheorie: Legitimationsbasis des Strafrechts oder dogmatisches Glasperlenspiel?* (Nomos 2003).

Helmholz R., 'Origins of the Privilege against Self-Incrimination: The Role of the European Ius Commune' [1990] New York University Law Review 962.

Herlin-Karnell E., *The Constitutional Dimension of European Criminal Law* (Hart Publishing 2012).

Hinarejos A., 'The Lisbon Treaty Versus Standing Still: A View from the Third Pillar' [2009] European Constitutional Law Review 99.

Hörnle T., '"Rights of Others" in Criminalisation Theory' in Simester A.P., du Bois-Pedain A. and Neumann U. (eds), *Liberal Criminal Law Theory, Essays for Andreas von Hirsch* (Hart Publishing 2014) 169.

Husak D., 'Social Engineering as an Infringement of the Presumption of Innocence: The Case of Corporate Criminality' [2014] Crim Law and Philos 353.

Husak D., *Overcriminalization: The Limits of the Criminal Law* (Oxford University Press 2008).

Igglezakis I., *The General Data Protection Regulation (Regulation 2016/679)* [in Greek] (Interactive Books 2018).

Jescheck H-H. and Weigend T., *Lehrbuch des Strafrechts: Allhemeiner Teil* (Duncker & Humblot 1996).

Kaiafa-Gbandi M., 'Coordinating organs in the fight against organised crime in the EU: From Police (Europol) to judicial (Eurojust) cooperation' [in Greek] [2003] Poiniki Dikaiosyni 165.

Kaiafa-Gbandi M., 'Case-law of the European Court of Justice and the new possibilities for EU intervention to the criminal law of Member States' [in Greek] [2006] Poiniki Dikaiosyni 476.

Kaiafa-Gbandi M., 'Current developments of criminal law in the EU and Rule of Law deficiencies' [in Greek] [2006] Poinika Chronika 577.

Kaiafa-Gbandi M., 'Preventing terrorism and the new pre-preventive criminal law: new crimes for combating crime in the EU' [in Greek] [2009] Poinika Chronika 385.

Kaiafa-Gbandi M., 'Surveillance models in the security state and fairness of criminal trial' in Kaiafa-Gbandi M. and Prittwitz C. (eds), *Surveillance and criminal repression in contemporary anti-crime policy* [in Greek] (Nomiki Bibliothiki 2011) 63.

Kaiafa-Gbandi M., 'The recent case-law of ECtHR on police entrapment and the right to a fair trial' [in Greek] [2011] Poiniki Dikaiosyni 59.

Kaiafa-Gbandi M., 'Supranational delineation of criminal repression: ideological developmental axes of EU criminal law' [in Greek] [2018] Poinika Chronika 497.

Kaiafa-Gbandi M., 'CJEU case law and the European Arrest Warrant: Fundamental directions and contemporary trends (Part A)' [in Greek] [2019] Poiniki Dikaiosyni 1.

Kaiafa-Gbandi M., 'CJEU case law and the European Arrest Warrant: Fundamental directions and contemporary trends (Part B)' [in Greek] [2019] Poiniki Dikaiosyni 153.

Kaiafa-Gbandi M., 'Information Exchange for the Purpose of Crime Control: the EU Paradigm for Controlling Terrorism—Challenges of an "Open" System for Collecting and Exchanging Personal Data' [2019] European Criminal Law Review 141.

Kaiafa-Gbandi M. and others, *DNA analysis and court practice* [in Greek] (Sakkoulas 2014).

Kaiafa-Gbandi M. and Papakyriakou T., *Elements of EU Criminal Law* [in Greek] (2nd edn, Sakkoulas 2019).

Kaisaris P. in Lampros Margaritis (ed), *Code of Criminal Procedure* [in Greek] (Nomiki Bibiliothiki 2011) 736.

Kalfelis G., 'Extraditing Greek Citizens' [in Greek] [2007] Poiniki Dikaiosyni 1188.

Karras A., *Code of Criminal Procedure* [in Greek] (3rd edn, Nomiki Bibiliothiki 2016).

Kedzior M., 'GDPR and beyond—a year of changes in the data protection landscape of the European Union' [2019] ERA Forum 505.

Kelleher D. and Murray K., *EU Data Protection Law* (Bloomsbury 2018).

Kietz D. and Maurer A., *From Schengen to Prüm. Deeper Integration through Enhanced Cooperation or Signs of Fragmentation in the EU?* (SWP Comments 2017) <www.swp-berlin.org/fileadmin/contents/products/comments/Com15_06_Ktz_Mrr_Ks.pdf> accessed on 3 February 2020.

Klimek L., *European Arrest Warrant* (Springer 2014).

Klip A., *European Criminal Law* (Intersentia 2016).

Konstantinidis A., *Criminal Procedure Law—Basic concepts* (Sakkoulas 2014).

Kostoris R.E. (ed), *Handbook on European criminal procedure* (Springer 2018) (*Handbook criminal procedure*).

Kostoris R.E. 'European Law and Criminal Justice' in Kostoris R.E. (ed), *Handbook on European criminal procedure* (Springer 2018) 3.

Kreissl R., 'Will More Data Bring More Security? Remarks on the Security Union Approach to Interoperability' in Carrera S. and Mitsilegas V. (eds), *Constitutionalising the Security Union* (CEPS 2017) 93.

Kuner C., 'International agreements, data protection and EU fundamental rights on the international stage: Opinion 1/15 (EU-Canada PNR) of the Court of Justice of the EU' [2018] Common Market Law Review 857.

Kuner C., 'Data Protection, Data Transfers, and International Agreements: the CJEU's Opinion 1/15' [2017] <https://verfassungsblog.de/data-protection-data-transfers-and-international-agreements-the-cjeus-opinion-115/> accessed 3 February 2020.

Kuskonmaz E. and Guild E., 'EU exclusive jurisdiction on surveillance related to terrorism and serious transnational crime, case review on opinion 1/15 of the CJEU' [2018] European Law Review 583.

Labayale H., 'The institutional framework' in Mitsilegas V., Bergström M. and Konstadinides T. (eds), *Research Handbook on EU Criminal Law* (Elgar 2016) 29.

Langbein J., 'The historical origins of the privilege against self-incrimination at common law' [1994] Michigan Law Review 1047.

Lima D., 'Criminalising Organised Crime on the *EU* Level: Understanding Crime through a Financial Aim Perspective?' in Ouwerkerk J. and other (eds), *The Future of EU Criminal Justice Policy and Practice—Legal and Criminological Perspectives* (Brill 2019) 161.

Linder A. (ed), *European Data Protection Law: General Data Protection Regulation 2016* (CreateSpace 2016).

Livos N., 'The procedural law position of those under suspicion to have committed a criminal offence' [in Greek] [1995] Poinika Chronika 1103.

Manoledakis I., *The legal interest as a fundamental concept of criminal law* [in Greek] (Sakkoulas 1998).

Manoledakis I., *Global Power and Legal Culture* [in Greek] (Sakkoulas 2005).

Manoledakis I., *Security and Freedom* [in Greek] (Sakkoulas 2002).

Margaritis L., 'Analysis and Coersion' in Margaritis L. and Kastanidou E. (eds), *DNA Analysis in criminal trial* [in Greek] (Nomiki Bibliothiki 2014) 119.

Margaritis L. and Kastanidou E. (eds), *DNA Analysis in criminal trial* [in Greek] (Nomiki Bibliothiki 2014).

Mitrou L., *The General Data Protection Regulation* [in Greek] (Sakkoulas 2017).

Mitsilegas V., 'The Constitutional Implications of Mutual Recognition in Criminal Matters in the EU' [2006] Common Market Law Review 1277.

Mitsilegas V., 'Constitutional Principles of the European Community and European Criminal Law' [2007] European Journal of Law Reform 301.

Mitsilegas V., 'The Borders Paradox: The Surveillance of Movement in a Union without Internal Frontiers' in Lindahl H. (ed), *A Right to Inclusion and Exclusion? Normative Fault Lines of the EU's Area of Freedom, Security and Justice* (Hart Publishing 2009) 33.

Mitsilegas V., 'The Transformation of Privacy in an Era of Pre-emptive Surveillance' [2015] Tilburg Law Review 35.

Mitsilegas V., *EU Criminal Law after Lisbon* (Hart Publishing 2016).

Mitsilegas V., 'The Security Union as a Paradigm of Preventive Justice: Challenges for Citizenship, Fundamental Rights and the Rule of Law' in Carrera S. and Mitsilegas V. (eds), *Constitutionalising the Security Union* (CEPS 2017) 5.

Mitsilegas V., 'European Criminal Law and the Dangerous Citizen' [2018] Maastricht Journal of European and Comparative Law 733.

Mitsilegas V., 'The European Model of Judicial Cooperation in Criminal Matters: Towards Effectiveness based on Earned Trust' [2019] Rev. Bras. de Direito Processual Penal 565.

Mitsilegas V., Bergström M. and Konstadinides T. (eds), *Research Handbook on EU Criminal Law* (Elgar 2016) (*Research Handbook*).

Morgan C., 'The European Arrest Warrant and Defendants' Rights: An Overview' in Blekxton R. and van Ballegooij W. (eds), *Handbook on the European Arrest Warrant* (Asser Press 2005) 195.

Muñoz de Morales Romero M., 'The taking account of EU previous sanctions in joint/accumulated punishment: the Spanish case' [2018] European Criminal Law Review 244.

Mylonopoulos C., 'Community Criminal Law and General Principles of Community Criminal Law' [in Greek] [2010] Poinika Chronika 161.

Nehl H.P., 'Article 48(1)—Presumption of Innocence' in Steve Peers and others, *The EU Charter of Fundamental Rights: A Commentary* (Hart Publishing 2014) 1278.

Papadamakis A., *Applications of Criminal Procedure* [in Greek] (Nomiki Vivltiothiki 2006).

Papadamakis A., 'Police entrapment: Limitations and transgressions' [in Greek] [2010] Poiniki Dikaiosyni 1326.

Papadamakis A., *Criminal Procedure* [in Greek] (8th edn, Sakkoulas 2018).

Papadamakis A., 'Issues concerning the Principle of Proportionality in Criminal proceedings' [in Greek] [2019] Poiniki Dikaiosyni 281.

Papaioannou Z., *Police law* [in Greek] (2nd edn, Sakkoulas 2005).

Papakyriakou T., *The principle of non self-incrimination in light of the recent case-law of the ECHR* (Nomiki Bibliothiki 2009).

Paraskevopoulos N., *Majorities in the Crosshairs—Terrorism and the Rule of Law* (Patakis 2003).

Paraskevopoulos N., *The foundations of criminal law—General Part: The criminal offence* [in Greek] (Sakkoulas 2008).

Pavlou S., 'The European Union and the ECHR' [in Greek] [2008] Poinika Chronika 97.

Peršak N., 'Using "Quality of Life" to Legitimate Criminal Law Intervention: Gauging Gravity, Defining Disorder' in Simester A.P., du Bois-Pedain A. and Neumann U. (eds), *Liberal Criminal Law Theory, Essays for Andreas von Hirsch* (Hart Publishing 2014) 225.

Roxin C., *Strafrecht Allgemeiner Teil Bd. 1* (C H Beck 2005).

Roxin C. and Schünemann B., *Strafverfahrensrecht* [29th edn, Beck 2017].

Satzger H., *International and European Criminal Law* (2nd edn, Beck 2018).

Shaw K., *The Court of Justice of the European Union: Subsidiary and Proportionality* (Brill Nijhoff 2018).

Sicurella R., 'EU competence in criminal matters' in Mitsilegas v., Bergström M. and Konstadinides T. (eds), *Research Handbook on EU Criminal Law* (Elgar 2016) 49.

Sieber U., 'The new architecture in Security Law: Crime control in the global risk society' in Sieber U. and others (eds), *Alternative Systems of Crime Control: National, Transnational, and International Dimensions* (Duncker & Humblot 2018) 3.

Sieber U. and others (eds), *Alternative Systems of Crime Control: National, Transnational, and International Dimensions* (Duncker & Humblot 2018) (*Alternative Systems*).

Simester A.P. and von Hirsch A., *Crimes, Harms, and Wrong* (Hart Publishing 2011).

Simester A.P., du Bois-Pedain A. and Neumann U. (eds), *Liberal Criminal Law Theory, Essays for Andreas von Hirsch* (Hart Publishing 2014) (*Liberal Criminal Law Theory*).

Sottiaux S., *Terrorism and the Limitation of Rights-The ECHR and the US Constitution* (Hart Publishing 2008).

Stewart H., 'The right to be presumed innocent' [2014] Crim Law and Philos 407.

Stumer A., *The Presumption of Innocence: Evidential and Human Rights Perspectives* (Hart Publishing 2010).

Symeonidou-Kastanidou E., 'Police violence: legislative framework and application issues' [in Greek] [2006] Nomiko Vima 1641.

Symeonidou-Kastanidou E., *Organised Crime and Terrorism* [in Greek] (Sakkoulas 2007).

Symeonidou-Kastanidou E., 'DNA Analysis and criminal trial: the European institutional framework' in Margaritis L. and Kastanidou E. (eds), *DNA Analysis in criminal trial* [in Greek] (Nomiki Bibliothiki 2014) 3.

Tadros V., 'The Ideal of the Presumption of Innocence' [2014] Crim Law and Philos 449.

Trebilcock M.J. and Daniels R.J., *Rule of Law Reform and Development: Charting the Fragile Path of Progress* (Edward Elgar Publishing 2008).

Trechsel S., *Human Rights in Criminal Proceedings* (Oxford 2005).

Triantafyllou G., 'The Principle of Proportionality in Criminal Proceedings' [in Greek] [1990] Elliniki Dikaiosyni 301.

Tsolka O., *The 'nemo tenetur se ipsum prodere/accusare' principle in the criminal trial* [in Greek] (PN Sakkoulas 2002).

Tsolka O., 'The right to non self-incrimination and the presumption of innocence' [in Greek] [2004] Poinika Chronika 97.

Tsolka O., 'Mutual recognition of criminal judicial decisions and protection of fundamental rights in the "area of freedom, security and justice" of the EU' [in Greek] [2018] Poinika Chronika 425.

Tzanetis A., 'The European Investigation Order (incorporating Directive 2014/41/EU by Law 4489/2017)' [in Greek] [2018] Poinika Chronika 81.

Tzanou M., *The Fundamental Right to Data Protection: Normative Value in the Context of Counter-Terrorism Surveillance* (Hart Publishing 2017).

Tzemos V., *The Charter of Fundamental Rights of the EU* [in Greek] (Nomiki Bibliothiki 2015).

Tzortzi V., *Personal Data Protection in the Area of Freedom, Security and Justice* [in Greek] (Nomiki Bibliothiki 2018).

Ugelvik S., *Police Cooperation and Sovereignty in the EU: Norway's Lessons for Europe* (*Transnational Criminal Justice*) (Routledge 2019).

Vavoula N., 'Prevention, Surveillance, and the Transformation of Citizenship in the "Security Union": The Case of Foreign Terrorist Fighters' [2018] Queen Mary School of Law Legal Studies Research Paper No. 293/2018.

Vedaschi A. and Graziani C., 'PNR Agreements between Fundamental Rights and National Security: Opinion 1/15' [2018] <http://europeanlawblog.eu/2018/01/23/pnr-agreements-between-fundamental-rights-and-national-security-opinion-115/> accessed 3 February 2020.

Vedaschi A. and Lubello V., 'Data Retention and its Implications for the Fundamental Right to Privacy; A European Perspective' [2015] Tilburg Law Review 14.

Vogiatzis P., The presumption of innocence (Article 6 para 2 ECHR) [in Greek] in Sisilianos L-A. (series dir) *European Convention on Human Rights, Article Commentary* [in Greek] (2nd edn, Nomiki Bibiliothiki 2017) 301.

Voigt P. and von dem Bussche A., *The EU General Data Protection Regulation (GDPR)—A Practical Guide* (Springer 2017).

Von Hirsch A., 'Der Rechtsgutsbegriff und das "Harm Principle"' [2002] Goltdammer's Archiv für Strafrecht 2.

Weigend T., 'Assuming that the Defendant Is Not Guilty: The Presumption of Innocence in the German System of Criminal Justice' [2014] Crim Law and Philos 285.

Weyembergh A., 'History of the Cooperation' in Kostoris R.E. (ed), *Handbook on European criminal procedure* (Springer 2018) 173.

Zachariadis A., 'Preventive body searches, the principle of proportionality and the protection of human dignity' [in Greek] [1995] Yperaspisi 1237.

Zimmermann F., Glaser S. and Motz A., 'Mutual recognition and its Implications for the Gathering of Evidence in Criminal proceedings: a Critical Analysis of the Initiative for a European Investigation Order' [2011] European Criminal Law Review 56.

www.ingramcontent.com/pod-product-compliance
Lightning Source LLC
Chambersburg PA
CBHW031330230926
51848CB00001B/166
9789004425224